DEDICATED TO MY CHILDREN
CLAUDETTE, CATHERINE,
EVERETT

AND TO THE
MEMORY OF MY
ELDEST SON ERWIN.

SEPTEMBER, 2015

Caribbean Chapters Publishing
P.O. Box 8050, Oistins, Christ Church, Barbados
www.caribbeanchapters.co

Editors:
Carol A. Pitt, Christina De Paris, Noreen Hillard,
Jane Silverman, Linda Libecape

ISBN (paperback): 978-151-7197-98-8

*My deepest gratitude to all who
helped me write this book.*

*Without the persistence of my son, Everett, the
original ten chapters would still be on a recovered
disk. He saw value in the first three chapters and
insisted that I finish the manuscript.*

*My volunteer editors: Christina De Paris, the
original editor, her willingness to read and give
feedback propelled me to finish the first draft.
Noreen Hillard's skills and patience lovingly
shaped and developed the manuscript.
Jane Silverman and Linda Libecape's keenness
and abilities contributed significantly to the
completion of it.*

*Finally, to my husband, who lovely supported me
when it seemed that all I was doing was writing.*

PROLOGUE

The flower of consciousness needs the mud out of which it grows.

- Eckhart Tolle -

I CHOSE to enter this universe in February 1948, and selected a wonderful teenaged girl as my mother. She was the eldest of five siblings whose mother died when she was four years old. I was never told I had a father and was oblivious to such a creature. When I became old enough to notice the murmur in the village: "isn't that child like Eglon?" I eventually figured out who my father was. I was like him in every way, very good-looking, dark-skinned and long-legged.

From my earliest recollection, life was not a bed of roses. I was born to a single mother in a colonized country that was very class- and color-conscious. Entrenched in the culture was the fact that a child born out of wedlock was designated a bastard, even though more than eighty percent of the children born during that period were born out of wedlock. Nevertheless for some Barbadians it was a shameful and embarrassing thing to happen. Perhaps this was as a result of the colonizers' religion, for in African culture before colonization, there was no bastard designation. To my mother I was a mistake of gross proportions. Can you imagine the kind of gestation I experienced? No wonder I have a propensity towards anxiety. According to Bruce Lipton, children come into this world with an insecure or secure attitude contributed by the mother's attitude during pregnancy.

What compounded my mother's situation was the fact that she became convinced that my father was not good enough for her. I was told that shortly after she became pregnant, he was sent to jail for stealing. Therefore he was considered undeserving of her, and she never spoke to him again. She later told me that her decision was fueled by the wagging tongues in the village who believed it was below her to be associated with him. Ma, which is what I called her, always said that my eldest son Erwin looked just like my father. Indeed, of my four children Erwin resembled me the most.

Erwin and I could both be considered rebels in society. We didn't easily follow. We saw through the façade of society and had difficulty following when we were not being led somewhere. I have to believe I am like my father, because all I have of my mother are her mannerisms. My mother was quiet and reserved, I am outgoing and bold. I therefore believe that my father was a very intelligent young man and with love, guidance and understanding he could have found his way in Barbados. He, before me, experienced a society 'so heavenly-minded it was no earthly good'. It's a society that if you veer in the slightest way from the so-called norms you are harshly judged and looked down upon—a society so small in size and understanding that it does not take much for you to become an outcast.

Eglon eventually migrated to Guyana where he married, had more children and lived as a law-abiding citizen.

I experienced the cruel reality of religious dogma that shaped the Barbadian society even before I was born. Ironically, the religious dogmas that shape most societies are believed to bring freedom to humans, but instead they are the very seed of the misery many of us experience.

I never got the opportunity to know my father. All my life I desired to meet him. In recent years, as I attempted to find him, I was eventually told by someone who grew up in his village in Guyana that he is dead. In fact, I was told that everyone in his village in Guyana believed he was from Africa. He never owned his Barbadian connection.

I saw him once when I was five years old. I vividly remember this tall man carrying a beautiful woven basket with a red toffee tin in it. I was on my way to my mother's workplace for lunch. We got an hour for lunch and many children went home. He lifted me up at the beginning of the gap where my mother's house still is today. Since he was a stranger to me, I cried until he put me down. I was walking with the older school girls. When we reached Ma's workplace and they told her what happened, these were my mother's words: "if he comes here, I am going to scald him."

When I was about fourteen years old we exchanged letters for a brief period. It is then that I learned that when he came when I was five years old, he was leaving for Guyana. My mother's great fear of me becoming like my father and his family kept me from knowing the other side of my family. I do communicate with a few of them now. My yearning to see him continued for years, due to my being told so often how much I look like him. When I would voice this desire to my mother's family they would merely say "Look in the mirror."

In all slave societies there developed among the slave class a very strong stratification. In Barbados, from my recollection, if you were lighter in complexion and your parents were married you had the greatest possibilities. If you were dark-skinned and your parents were married you had more opportunity than the dark-skinned child who was a bastard. If you were light-skinned or mulatto, even though a bastard, you had more opportunity than the dark-skinned legitimate child and the dark-skinned bastard. So the dark-skinned bastard was always at the bottom of the societal ladder. Contributing to the opportunities of the mulatto bastard was the fact that many times the families on either the mother's or father's side, more often the father, were in a better position to make opportunities possible for the child. I am a very dark-skinned bastard. Therefore I came into this world with all the odds against me. In spite of this fact and the fact that I was such a mistake in my mother's eyes, I entered this world with a determined spirit.

In my mind I always felt that given the opportunity I would do as well as or better than anyone. The journey has been a long one. Many who admired me from afar and thought that I was very self-confident, after getting to know me, were amazed at my self-doubt. Contributing to this debilitating self-doubt were the very negative experiences of my childhood. I developed doubt in my ability and a hatred for my looks, particularly my long, skinny legs. I distinctly remember being called a blackbird. I guess to the accuser, I resembled the blackbird of Barbados. They are jet black with long, spindly legs.

My legs were the subject of much ridicule, even by my family. I clearly recall an incident that happened shortly after Barbados was damaged by hurricane Janet in 1956. My great aunt, who lived in the United States, sent a barrel with goodies for the family. I can clearly remember the negative comments made by one of my mother's sisters about my inability to wear shorts because my legs were so skinny. Oh! If grown-ups could be more cognizant of the damage they do to tender minds with their careless words. Often adults repeat words to children they would think twice about before saying to other adults. This is because most of them neither recognize nor respect the individuality of children. In elementary school I was so thin and long-legged that some students repeated this rhyme when they saw me: "bones in the ally, ten for a penny."

This book is about the path my life has taken from childhood in a little village in Barbados to where I am today. The experiences and encounters along that path were as knives in a sculptor's hands, shaping me into understanding the spirit BEING that I am. The rape, the molestation, my unconscious family, the mean headmistress, the unwise shopkeeper, the encouraging headmistress, the wise church elder who recognized my ability, the many hours left alone, the rejection by family and friends, teenaged motherhood, migration to

America, the raising of four children on a shoestring budget, divorce, a bout with clinical depression, all these and much more have been my teachers. As Florence Schovel Schinn states in her book The Wisdom of Florence Schovel Schinn: "No man is my enemy, no man is my friend, all men are my teachers." I will broaden that by saying all life experiences are my teachers.

Like me there are many men, women and children struggling to negotiate this school called life. It is made even more complex by the man-made dogmas of our society. My hope is that the readers of these pages will find inspiration and encouragement as they search to find who they are and have been all along.

ONE

Childhood

*If you want to save the world, you
have to save the children.*

- Luciano -

*What if we thought of family less as a determining influence
by which we are formed and more the raw material from
which we can make life?*

- Thomas Moore -

I WAS but a small child when my mother joined Gentles' Pentecostal Church. Finding herself pregnant shortly after her grandmother's death, feeling all alone and very ashamed, she found solace in the church. My earliest recollection of life has to do with going to church. She made that decision then, and I can declare she never looked back. She continued to be faithful to what she believed to be truth. Her example of faithfulness to what she believed significantly impacted my life. I grew up believing in a vengeful, literal God—a God who accepted only people who acted and dressed a certain way; a God who was waiting, ready and willing to punish for the slightest infraction. I literally believed that God lived above the blue sky and that hell was just beneath the earth. Consequently I learned very early to harshly judge others and myself. My indoctrination left no room for grey areas, my understanding was colored black or white. In my recollection I spent many hours in church. The church held many revival meetings with the intent of converting lost souls. Many nights I went to sleep lying on the church pew as my mother and Uncle Moses fervently worshipped their lord.

Uncle Moses was my mother's youngest brother. He was so named because his mother died when he was just a few days old. My grandmother was only 27 years old when she died, leaving five children. My mother was the eldest. After her was another girl, then twins, and then Uncle Moses. By the time I came along the only grandparent alive was my great-grandfather, Papa. He was the father of my mother's father. He and his wife raised my mother and her siblings because their father died at a young age also. You probably wonder what happened to the grandparents on their mother's side. My grandmother, I was told, was almost white. There was not a single picture of her to be seen. In fact, one of the women in the village told me that when my grandfather married Sadie Harper, it was rumored around the village: "come see the white woman Joe Reid married." My grandmother was a mulatto woman who fell in love with a very handsome, tall, dark-skinned man, a tailor who knew how to dress. He was well-liked by the ladies and as a result my grandmother's 'higher' class, her family disowned her when she married him.

My journey home on those long nights of revival was usually on Uncle Moses' back as they walked the short distance from the church to Mrs. Hinkson's house. Since I was being raised to be a good Christian, when I became old enough I went to three different Sunday Schools: on Sunday mornings with Mrs. Hinkson to the Pilgrim Holiness Church, in the mid-morning to the Pentecostal Sunday school, and in the evening to the Moravian one with my cousins. As a good Christian girl I could never wear jewelry, go to the movies, listen to cultural calypso music, play cards, go to carnival, or pitch marbles—pitching marbles was considered a boy's game.

It was in the church that my natural ability and sharpness of mind was first evident. When the church presented special programs at Christmas, Mother's Day and harvest time, I was taught poems, which we called 'recitations'. I memorized them and then I stood before the congregation and confidently recited them. In Sunday school my hand shot up quickly as I was always ready to answer any question the teacher asked. Those were the innocent days and the happiest days of my life.

In the 1950s, Barbados was not far removed economically from the days of slavery, even though slavery had been abolished in 1839. Sugarcane was still king of crops and the majority of unskilled labor was associated with harvesting the sugarcane. It was a lucrative way for the unskilled to get ahead. Many men and women were able to build and own a small home as a result of working in the sugar industry. For many, labor work during the crop season was the only regular work they could get. To my understanding, my family was from the artisan or house slave class. Neither my mother nor her sister ever worked in the fields. They both worked in the great house at Husbands' plantation as domestics. Their brother worked at Husbands also. Since he was a mechanic, he repaired and drove the lorries. In British vocabulary a lorry is a flatbed truck.

My great grandparents' house is one of the two places I spent my time when I was small. It was between two plantations, Wanstead and Husbands. Husbands was the more active of the two. At that time my great grandparents' house was the second last house in Hinds Hill, part of the larger village called Cave Hill. My great grandfather's house was so close to Husbands that as a child I would watch the organized system of reaping the sugarcane. I imagine this system was much the same as it was during the days of enslavement. One group of men cut down the sugarcane with cutlasses; another group tied them in bundles and the heavy bundles were then loaded onto the heads of women. The women then climbed a ladder and dumped the bundles on the lorry.

My clearest memory of my mother working as a domestic was when she worked for the mulatto school teacher in our village. I can still remember the abundance of the lady's kitchen; abundance that I most often only saw and smelled. My mother's boss had a niece who was my age. She came into this world under similar circumstances as me, but she was different. She had a lighter complexion and her father's family was from a different class. We attended the same primary school and sometimes we would play together.

The memory of a particular day is still vivid. One of her school friends came to visit. This is a girl I was acquainted with, since we all attended the same school, but she was not my friend. I played with them that day and when lunch time came I was allowed to sit at the table with them. However, the little dark servant girl had to eat with a spoon while the others ate with knife and fork. Maybe I should have been grateful that they allowed me to eat at the table. Even at that young age—I was no older than five—that differentiation had its impact. I knew within myself that if they could eat with knife and fork, I could too. From a very young age I had a sense of being capable of doing anything anyone else could do.

The best thing about my mother's work in the village was the fact that I got to see her. Although I have fond memories of visiting and eating at her workplace, there were also days I was not allowed to visit. On one of those days I was left alone at Mrs. Hinkson's house. A rustling in the things stored on the canopy above the bed made me imagine that there was a centipede among them. Centipedes were common visitors in chattel houses. I became lonely and afraid and I ran to my mother. Instead of being welcomed, I was whipped and sent back. Maybe Ma thought I was inappropriately dressed to be visiting, for I grew up with much emphasis on personal appearance. One had home clothes, church clothes, school clothes and grown-ups had town clothes. Although sometimes you only had one outfit for each place, because your clothes were designated, this guaranteed that you were always clean and tidy. I am sure I was wearing home clothes when I visited.

When I started school sometimes I would go to my mother's workplace for my lunch, or I would see my mother when she took her boss's lunch to the school. Eventually that would change as my mother left that job in her quest for better pay and better working conditions. In time she worked as a live-in domestic, which meant I saw very little of her. I can now imagine the difficulty of my mother's life as she struggled to support herself and me on a meager salary. In those days domestic servants worked seven days a week for as little as five dollars. My mother's live-in job left me at the mercies of relatives. Consequently, very early I came to believe that no one can take the place of a mother in a child's life. It is true that I was among family, but really there was no one that was mine. My cousins had their mothers and each other. I had no sibling and no parent. I was fed, my clothes were washed, I was beaten when I did something wrong; but in reality, I was not nurtured.

I was my mother's only child for seventeen years and the eldest among the cousins. I spent many of my first twelve years living between two homes. I spent the daytime with my aunts and my seven cousins at Papa's house and I slept with Uncle Moses and Mrs. Hinkson at her house. At that time, Papa's house was one of the largest houses in the village. Before America changed its emigration laws in 1924, Papa worked for many years in New York. With his migration money he bought many pieces of land and built a nice house. Papa was not alone in this, for migration played a significant role in the economic development of all the Caribbean islands.

However, he built his house on the land his wife inherited. Perhaps it was because her land was located on what would be considered a main road. I often wondered how her parents became so well off. She was born in the late 1800s and her parents not only had land, but owned an upstairs wall house. This is another reason why I believe they were of the artisan class, for it was not possible for a chattel slave to own so much in such a short time after emancipation.

On the land surrounding the house there were a great variety of fruit trees. There were mango, soursop, avocado pear, breadfruit, ackee* dunks*, paw paw and tamarind trees. When ackees and dunks were in season we filled our stomachs with the sweet fruit. We ate the sour ones too when there was nothing else to eat. The eating of the mangoes, paw paws, sugar apples, and pears were controlled by the adults, for they were often stored to ripen. Occasionally we would find a fallen ripe mango ready to eat. What a delicious treat that would be. Food was not that plentiful; there were no kitchen cupboards containing packaged snacks.

Often for breakfast I received a cup of tea and a few biscuits or a piece of bread. Many times hot cereals such as cream of wheat, sago, cornmeal pap, oatmeal were available, but back then I detested cooked cereal. During the day it was no use telling anyone you were hungry, because you grew up knowing that one cooked meal a day was all that was available. When school was in session, we were given lunch and we ate our big meal in the evening. As children we appreciated the ripe berries and fruit when in season.

Rice was the main staple, with soup, cou cou and 'stew food' interchangeably eaten. With the exception of stew food, I now relish these Barbadian dishes. Stew food in Barbados was made by cooking a combination of root vegetables, with breadfruit when available, and dumplings. In my family the stew food dumplings were made lighter than the soup dumplings by adding baking powder. It was more regularly served with salted cod gravy. The only part of that meal I liked was the dumplings. Cou cou, the cornmeal and okra combination served with flying fish gravy when flying fish was in season, was no favorite of mine either. This dish is now Barbados' national dish.

Rice I ate. However, my family never cooked white rice. We always combined it with something. Peas and beans were favored. Determined not to cook what we call plain rice, cabbage leaves, okra, spinach, or pumpkin was added to give the rice more food value and flavor. Pea soup, flavored with a small portion of meat, was my favorite. Many times the same root vegetables in stew food were in the soup. Again, my favorite part was the dumplings. Meat was served once a week. In addition to flying fish when in season and salted cod fish, the other protein staples were red herring, canned corned beef and canned fish. When Scott Peck in his book *The Road Less Travelled* talked about delayed gratification I readily got the point, for I had practiced it many times. Sunday was the day we were served some kind of meat, usually chicken or beef. I would eat everything in my bowl, in the meantime relishing the taste of that small piece of meat. I was never disappointed.

Work was also part of our childhood. As we got older, each of us had responsibilities. We had morning chores and evening chores, with fewer chores on school days. One responsibility was to keep the yard around the house spotless. When there were chickens in the chicken coop, we were responsible for cleaning under the chicken coop. We made our own brooms from a plant we called rock sage, and as we swept the yard the brooms produced a sweet aroma. The girls did the dishes and swept the house. We did not have store-bought Brillo or dishwashing liquid in those days, but our dishes and pots were immaculate from the supplies we used. We used the ends of soap left from the block of laundry soap along with the rough bark from coconut trees and a little marl—fine white sediment of a certain kind of stone—to make those pots squeaky clean. Having responsibilities throughout childhood prepared us to become responsible adults.

As I think about it now, it seems like the girls

had more chores than the boys. However, the boys were always tending to sheep, goats, cows, at least one pig, and sometimes rabbits. The boys handled the livestock more, but I remember going with them in search of grass and certain bushes for the animals. We called this 'finding meat' for the animals. As mentioned before, as we did this in the summer months, we found and ate whatever was edible. When it was crop season we went to the already reaped sugarcane fields and mash trash. Barbadians call the dry discarded cane leaves that literally covered the fields 'trash'. We would use our feet to locate any leftover cane under the trash. When a good piece was found, we peeled it with our teeth and delightfully sucked the sweet sugarcane juice.

We had plenty of space to play and many trees to climb. The marks on my shins are evidence of this outdoor romping. If we wanted toys, we made them. We played shop using the leaves and the dirt and even the slugs for meat. The boys in particular ingeniously used sticks and string to set birds traps. We made our own kites from any large piece of paper that we could find. Wanstead plantation across the street became a brick manufacturing factory, so the boys would acquire the discarded large bags that had contained cement to make big kites. The kites were pasted together with the sticky fruit from the clammy cherry tree. There was a large tree in Papa's yard, so we were never short of glue.

The boys made rollers by pushing old bicycle tires along with a piece of wood. Boys made exact replicas of the lorries that transported the sugarcane and they used the sugarcane peelings to load their lorries. Some boys in the village replicated the lorries with amazing precision. Another toy that the boys made was a scooter, very similar to the modern day version that costs so much in stores today. The main frame was made from wood and the wheels were made from empty pint milk tins. I also learned to make rags dolls, but I did that at Mrs. Hinkson's house with her neighbor's children. In those days playing was time-consuming, because you had to use your imagination to create what you wanted to play with.

The days with my aunts and cousins were innocent, and not so innocent times. Wanstead plantation was directly across the street from

Papa's house. I never knew when Wanstead was primarily a sugar-producing plantation. Most plantations were owned by descendants of the white planter class, but Wanstead was one of the few owned by a person of African descent. Mr. Moore was a dark-skinned, enterprising man. He always had one or two operations going on at Wanstead. The biggest one I can remember was the rock-crushing cement block factory. At one time there was a joiner shop* run by two brothers by the side of the cement block factory. Consequently, there were always many young men in close proximity to our house. The two who worked in the joiner shop were probably around the same age as my aunts and uncle. Therefore they became friendly with my family.

My cousins and I would visit the joiner shop sometimes. I must explain that the work area was not closed in; anyone passing the street would see the young men at work, but there was a room where the tools were stored. The details in my mind are sketchy, but when I was eight years old the taller of the two brothers raped me. This was the first of many traumatic incidents of my childhood. The name of the man escapes me. He was an adult, I was a child.

Yet the night when my aunt told my mother, Ma beat me severely. This entrenched the self-doubt that plagued me for years. When it happened I kept it a secret. My clothes were the revealing evidence.

There was no one with whom I had an intimate relationship. Intimacy between parent and child, and between children and adults was not the norm. Children were fed and clothed. They were to be seen and not heard. What a violation of the human spirit! Oh! If adults would only understand that children are not extensions of them, but unique little persons, fully packaged, having much to offer when they come into this world and only needing guidance to become their true selves. I had no knowledge of sex. He opened up a whole new world to me. Nevertheless, I was made to feel guilty and thus the foundation of self-hate and self-reproach was laid.

I have encountered many children who exude neediness. I know because I was one of those little children. A little girl so needy is always an easy target for unconscious men. The rape occurred shortly after I had experienced my first loss. Uncle Moses, whom I was so close to, migrated to England. He had to do so in order make a life for himself. This did not nullify the fact that his absence created a great hole in my heart. Only as I matured did it dawn on me that this too was a traumatic experience for me. He was only thirteen years older than me, but we were close. He had become my father figure.

I played with my cousins at Papa's house in the daytime and travelled to Mrs. Hinkson's house in the evening. It was at Mrs. Hinkson's single-unit wooden chattel house where Uncle Moses, my mother and I lived. When Ma was working at Husbands she would fetch me and we would walk home together. When she started working farther away and sleeping on the job, I made the trek by myself. I had the choice of two ways to go to Mrs. Hinkson's house. Either along the main street, or the shorter route over the hill. Over the hill, however, was a fairly perilous place for a little girl to walk by herself.

Mrs. Hinkson was a distant cousin whose mother also died when she was a baby. She was raised by her aunt, my great-grandmother, who raised my mother and her siblings, which created a close connection. Mrs. Hinkson would always say: "I am so grateful for my aunt who sent me to school." She was born at a time when many children, even those who had parents, went to work on a plantation instead of going to school. Mrs. Hinkson demonstrated her gratitude by doing all she could for my mother and her siblings. According to my aunt, when they were growing up, sometimes the only food they had to eat was from Mrs. Hinkson's kitchen.

The only family I knew was polarized along religious lines. Those that lived at Papa's house were not very religious. They attended James Street Methodist Church. Historically, it was established after much persecution by the mother church—the Anglican or Church of England. Those of us at Mrs. Hinkson's house attended churches that had stricter guidelines. Mrs. Hinkson attended the Pilgrim Holiness, and Uncle Moses, Ma and I attended the Pentecostal church.

These holiness churches were allowed on the island many years after the Anglican and the Methodist churches. Their form of worship was more dramatic, particularly the Pentecostal churches. It was a sight to see when the members, especially women, became filled with the Holy Spirit, or as we would say in those days: 'got in the power'. My mother was one of these women. People would gather around these churches just to see the members 'get in the power'. They would jump and shake and sometimes they would even fall on the floor. While the Anglican, Methodist and Catholic Churches allowed their members freedom of choice in dress and socialization, I was reared with the restrictions of the fire and brimstone churches.

Mrs. Hinkson was one of the few people I have experienced who lived what she professed. She was married to a blacksmith who died long before I was born. I never saw her with a man. She was like a grandmother to me. In fact, she was a grandmother to the whole village. She worked very hard at the hospital as a washer woman. One can only imagine the magnitude of that work, for there were no washing machines then. Her salary may not have been large, but it was regular and she was content.

She was also happy to give. I learned from her the art of giving. She gave, and she gave and she gave. She gave to her family, neighbors and friends, but she gave most to her church. I can still remember the missionary box she filled and turned in every quarter year in addition to her weekly offering. It was only after her death at age ninety-eight that we understood the scope of her giving. It was then that we learned about the fathers who would borrow to support their families when they were short of cash. Many times I witnessed her calling to the children of her friends as they passed by her house, asking them if they wanted something to eat. The only food many people ate some days was from Mrs. Hinkson's kitchen.

As the grandmother I never had, she fed me and kept me in pretty dresses and needed shoes. She was the only help my mother had in providing for my needs. She made my Christmas special. How vividly I remember going with her to the dressmaker on Christmas Eve night to get our Christmas dresses. A very important tradition in Barbados was getting new church clothes; women's and girls' dresses were always white. Many of the unchurched got new clothes just so they could attend church on Christmas morning. While many went without, Ma could depend on Mrs. Hinkson to provide for me.

In addition to church, we went many places together. Our big adventure was going on church excursions. Excursions were big events, particularly for those with lower economic status. Before there were so many cars in Barbados, churches would hire buses once a year. For a fee you would go with a group to one of the many beautiful scenic spots such as Foul Bay, Bathsheba, the Crane, and Bath. Without these excursions, these places that are enjoyed by tourists would only be places many Barbadians heard about.

Picnic baskets were usually packed with sandwiches, baked chicken, pudding (pound cake) sweet drinks (soda), macaroni and cheese, and rice and peas. They took food to the excursion that was not the regular daily fare. Hence, in addition to the bus ride, children looked forward to the special food. Usually the buses would be packed. One excursion is especially memorable. I could see my new dress now. It had a white background with red parasols printed all over it. However, I never got to wear it. A late-comer trying to find a seat on the bus spilled her greasy gravy all over my beautiful dress. Luckily we were close to home, therefore I returned home and changed. As the buses journeyed to the destination many people sang church songs and beat their cymbals. An excursion was indeed a happy, carefree experience.

The first time the evangelist Billy Graham came to Barbados, I went with Mrs. Hinkson to hear him. I had never experienced so many people in one place. I was too young to comprehend what he was saying and I certainly don't remember a word he said. What I do remember about that night is that when we arrived home, late as it was, we had to tend to a sheep that had given birth. Mrs. Hinkson's sheep was my responsibility during the day. This was during the period when Ma was sleeping on the job away from the village. I travelled to Mrs. Hinkson's house for lunch and on my lunch break I moved and watered the sheep. I was no more than eight or nine.

Mrs. Hinkson had a beautiful voice. I still can't carry a tune, but one of our favorite pastimes was singing her favorite songs. At times we would lie on her bed; these were the days after she had retired. We lay in opposite directions on the bed. I had the hymn book. She did not need it because she knew every song by heart. I usually chose the songs. She never minded that I could not carry a tune. Her favorite was *Great Is Thy Faithfulness.* She often sang solos in church. Every time I hear that song, I can hear her clearly singing it.

She took retirement very hard. She was still strong and hated to stop working. She was old enough and was forced to quit. Not very long after she quit work she developed tuberculosis and was hospitalized for months. This was an empty time for me. I had gotten used to her being there. Then I was left up to my own devices once again.

After she came home from the hospital, Ma and I continued to live with her. Even after Ma got married we lived with her until Ma built her own house next door. Ma cared for Mrs. Hinkson for years until she died at age 98, on January 10th, 1995. One morning when Ma took over her breakfast, she found her dead. She died peacefully in her sleep. I had planned a trip home and was excited about taking my first two grandchildren for her to see. We travelled, but instead we were there for her memorial service. Many relatives from Canada and America came home for her going away celebration; indeed it was a celebration. We celebrated her life with many of the beautiful hymns she loved to sing. My oldest daughter played the piano. 'Hinkda' would have liked that, because my daughter had become 'her girl'. She became Hinkda when Claudette was unable to pronounce her name. Hinkda was an awesome role model. She lived a peaceful, contented life. She was contented with so little. Contrary to modern times, it never dawned on her that because she was making more money and her house was paid for she needed a bigger one. To her it just meant she had more to give. What an amazing life of Ubuntu*.

Her heart eventually failed, but even in her final moments her mind was sharp. She could recite long verses of scripture backward up to the time of her death. I remember that as she and I passed in the street, young and old would call to her and she would respond, "God bless you." The proverbs and aphorisms I came to understand as part of our African heritage, she often repeated to make a point. When she referred to my not being in school, she would say, "you can carry a cow to water, but you can't make him drink." In other words she believed I was given every opportunity. And when she believed I was sexually active her words were, "what sweeten goat mouth will burn his tail."

In my early days, Uncle Moses was the only male I had a paternal relationship with. Ma, the eldest and he, the youngest, had a special bond. I think it was helped by the fact that they belonged to the same religion. As I mentioned, my earliest recollection of him was associated with church. I also remember coming home from school to Mrs. Hinkson's house, and for a short while he was there to greet me. One day when I got home from school there was much commotion because he had fallen asleep while cooking and burned down Mrs. Hinkson's kitchen. If the kitchen were attached to the house, the house would have burned also. In those days in Barbados many cooked over fire hearths. Uncle Moses was lying in bed reading his bible and fell into a deep sleep. In his words, "I got saved when I was a young man." As small as I was, I can remember his seriousness about serving his Lord. I overheard many a conversation between him and Brother Luke about receiving the Holy Spirit and speaking in tongues. He will be 81 this year (2015) and he is still a fervent believer.

Although his grandmother wanted him to learn the carpenter's trade, he found no affinity to it. Therefore he eventually joined the droves of immigrants who left the island in the 1950s to seek their fortunes. Migration to places of opportunity was a significant aspect of the economic development of many of the Caribbean Islands. Often men and women migrated to the colonizing country or the so-called 'mother country'. Unlike many of the other Caribbean islands, England was the only mother country Barbados ever had. However, many Barbadians worked on the Panama Canal, the oil fields in Trinidad, and some even worked in Cuba. During the 1950s hundreds of men and women left Barbados for England; women to study nursing and men to work for London Transport. Needless to say, I missed him terribly.

With my mother working as a live-in domestic and Uncle Moses gone, I spent many hours alone at Mrs. Hinkson's house. When school was in session, Mrs. Hinkson went to work at 7 a.m. Therefore I was alone until I left for school, which started at 9 a.m. I came home to an empty house for lunch. I often did not eat because the food was cold. Perhaps in a loving, caring environment I would have been happy to eat what was provided. When school was out for the day, I would change my clothes at Mrs. Hinkson's house and then trek to Papa's house. The food there was cooked earlier in the day and was always room temperature. To this day I do not care for cooked food that is room temperature. Later in the evening I would return to sleep at Mrs. Hinkson's.

Since I spent so much time alone, when I got ill it was no different. Imagine a young girl between the ages of nine and eleven being left alone so often. Usually my aunt would send my food by a male cousin, but that was the extent of my care. The sickness I remember clearly was mumps. Oh how painful it was! Who was there during the day to comfort me or offer me a drink? No one. During the day I stayed in that house alone until I was better. Again, I was in a very vulnerable situation, but I had the presence of mind to deny the advances of he who brought me the food. Years later, I had to put the self-righteous individual in his place when he started to tell me how bad I was when I was young. Being left on my own at an early age, I learned to make my own decisions. As a result, I am strongly opposed to leaving children alone. I know the dangers of leaving children alone, particularly girls. I also know that the smarter and more aware a child is, the less you want to leave them alone and unoccupied.

TWO

School Days

No mo Latin, no mo, French, no mo licks to mek cry,
No mo wata to drop outta muh eye.

EDGEHILL WAS the girls' primary school in Cave Hill, St. Michael. This school, along with Montgomery boys' school, were Moravian Schools. The Moravian Protestant Church was the earliest church to break away from Catholicism. They arrived in Barbados in 1732. Wherever they built a church, they started a school. They converted the enslaved and also educated them. When I started going to school at the age of five, Ma was still working for the mulatto lady in our village. Ma's boss was also the infants' A and B/kindergarten teacher at Edgehill.

How well I remember that first morning

on my way to school. We stopped for shelter from the rain under a shop awning, and while sheltering it was discovered that I had my shoes on the wrong feet. I can still remember the embarrassment of that moment. I don't know how long it lasted, but in the beginning I walked the two thirds of a mile to and from school with Ma's boss. At lunch time I walked home with the older girls.

At Edgehill every student wore a navy blue jumper and a white blouse. The economic status of the students was evident by what was on their feet. Those whose parents were better off wore shoes; those whose parents had limited funds wore pumps—Ked shoes. Wearing Keds engendered a negative response. These were the days before sneakers became fashionable and expensive. Then there were the students who came barefooted. I started in shoes. Perhaps it was my mother's employer who provided them. Eventually my footwear reflected my mother's economic status, and I wore pumps. Many times my shoes were provided by Mrs. Hinkson, especially when she observed that my shoes had holes.

My early days at Edgehill conjure up pleasant

memories, in spite of the fact that we were punished for the slightest infraction. The headmistress had a long strap coiled up on her desk and she did not hesitate to put it down our backs. We got spanked for being late for school. Some teachers spanked us hard across our open hands or knuckles with rulers. However, when time allowed we would play and jump and skip to our hearts' content in the school yard. The older board and shingle building that was Edgehill Girls' Primary had been a one-room school house when my mother and her sisters went there. When I attended, it had a brick addition that contained 3 classrooms. The lower grades, K-3, were housed in the older section, while the higher grades, 4-8, were in the newer section.

A typical day at Edgehill began with assembly. A teacher read a scripture and the students sang a prayer. At lunch time before we left for home we blessed our food by saying grace. When we returned we gave thanks before we started. In the evening before dismissal at 3 pm, we sang another hymn. The hymn that conjures up those school day memories began with the following verse: 'Day is dying in the west, Heaven *is touching earth with rest...*' Although Edgehill Primary, by the time I attended, was a public school, worship continued to be an integral part of the school day. I can still repeat many of the Bible passages I learned at Edgehill Primary.

We learned the basics of reading, writing and arithmetic by rote or mental work. We had to commit everything to memory and be able to give the right answer when randomly called upon, or we got licks*. I did really well in my early days of schooling. Perhaps it was because the mulatto lady was my teacher and she favored me. I learned fast, but my handwriting was horrible. I can remember being hit across my fingers because my writing was so bad. My cursive writing hasn't improved much. We memorized the parts of speech and we learned our times tables backward and forwards.

We wrote on what we called slates. A slate was a piece of slate about twelve to fifteen inches long and about ten inches wide, set in a wooden frame. Usually we wrote on the slate what we were learning at that time and erased it and made the slate clean for the next time. Exercise books came later. They served a two-fold purpose. We wrote in them and on the back were many of the basic principles of arithmetic. We differentiated between the pencil we used to write on slates by calling the slate one 'pencil' and the one with the wooden casing 'lead pencil'. In the higher grades there were pens with removable nibs. On each desk was an ink well. You dipped your pen in the ink well as you wrote. We also spilled ink on the desk and at the end of the school year we had to scrub our desks. We scrubbed those desks with white sagebush and marl. You never saw such clean desks!

I continued to attend Edgehill Primary for a while after Ma stopped working for the mulatto lady in the village. I would then go back and forth to school with the bigger girls. Mrs. Hinkson's house was half a mile from the school. Those were adventurous days. The bigger girls would raid people's ackee and mango trees as we travelled to and from school. They particularly liked to raid Mr. Bass' mango trees which were behind his house. Mr. Bass was a very tall mulatto man who it was rumored was mad. The very sight of him made us scamper. We also ran very fast when we believed we were going to be late for school.

Usually two bells were rung in the morning and after lunch. If we were not at school when the first bell rung, we would run for dear life to get there before the second bell sounded. We knew that licks* were the consequence of being late. We were not allowed excuses; we were expected to be on time all the time.

Another Edgehill memory is the mid-morning break when we were given biscuits and milk. They usually mixed powdered milk with tap water and served it. There was no hot and cold water tap. I can still taste that milk. I particularly liked the excess dry milk we were given at the end of the school year. It was messy to eat, but it sure tasted sweet.

I will also never forget the day Edgehill Primary was swarmed by bees. Edgehill, as it was rightly named, was situated on the edge of a hill. Under the hill was a cave, thus giving the village I lived in the name Cave Hill. The hill overlooked the village of Grazettes. Out of the blue one afternoon, the beehive in the gully was disturbed and the bees swarmed the school, causing pandemonium for a short while. I was not stung, but I heard that Ms. Wells, a teacher from the village, was severely stung. School was dismissed early that day.

Another unforgettable experience happened when I was attending Edgehill Primary. One morning on my way to school I met my mother's oldest brother, Sam, who gave me all of his pocket change. I went into Hank's shop, which was on the opposite side of the road, directly across from Edgehill. I went to buy one 'pully candy'. This candy was the length of licorice and the consistency of taffy and covered in paper like a salt water taffy. I knew that it cost a penny. Barbados had a coin worth two cents called a penny.

I had the penny in one hand and the rest of the money grasped tightly in the other hand. The shopkeeper, Hank's mother, opened my other hand, counted my money and gave me pullies for every cent I had. I went to school with a handful of candy and was severely chided by the teacher, who used to be my mother's boss. I still remember the feeling of being powerless. First, I was unable to tell the shopkeeper I only needed one, and then I had to endure the severe judgmental scolding from the mulatto lady for something I did not intend to do. I had no voice as a child. If I had had a voice I would have been able to explain to her what had happened and perhaps she would have heard me. Adults, in failing to value the individual spirits of children, inflict much pain in their hearts.

I would be amiss not to mention the only white couple, Mr. and Mrs. Shepherd, who lived close to Edgehill. They owned a shop that sold a variety of necessities, from needles and thread to school supplies. We depended upon Mrs. Shepherd's shop when we lost our pencils or needed an eraser. To us children, the most sought after things Mrs. Shepherd sold were ice cream blocks. She froze delicious, milky concoctions of various flavors like mango, coconut and soursop, in ice trays and sold a block for a penny. Getting a penny to buy an ice cream block from Mrs. Shepherd was the greatest treat that we enjoyed all school year.

I did well in the mulatto lady's class. However, as I got to the higher classes I began to have problems. I was very curious as a child and I still am. Curiosity is a sign of intelligence. The headmistress at Edgehill thought I was like the child in the poem 'Meddlesome Matty', which was penned by Ann Taylor and published in 1883. It seemed to me that my name, Elaine

Reid, was needlessly called when there was a problem. I felt I was accused of many things I was not guilty of. The straw that broke the camel's back was when I was accused of stealing a geography book. The book was later found in a cabinet. My mother had had enough, so she moved me to St. John the Baptist Girl's School in Thorpes, St. James.

The parish of St. James was next to St. Michael. Barbados is divided into eleven parishes, each named after a church saint. The distance from Papa's house to my new school was about four miles, hence I travelled to school by bus. St. John the Baptist was an Anglican school. Like the Moravians, it was now a public school. The color of my uniform was now a white shirt under a burgundy jumper. The school day started and ended much like Edgehill Primary. The only difference was, we attended church service once a week. I believe this was because the church was next door to the school. This was my first exposure to the formal worship in the Anglican church. It was so different from the emotionalism of the Pentecostal church that I was accustomed to. The one thing I remember learning at St. John the Baptist girls' school was the poem 'Rover in Church'. All I can remember is *"It is better late than never you know. Besides, I waited an hour or so, I couldn't get them to open the door."*

Ms. Clark, the headmistress at St. John the Baptist, was one of the few women who owned a car. She passed by Papa's house and often she would give me a ride. Unlike the headmistress at Edgehill, she expressed confidence in me. I no longer went home for lunch and would never forget the lunch time when I was being my curious self. While the other children were outside playing, I was in the school reading everything that was posted on the blackboards. Instead of chiding me, she made a positive remark about my ability to learn. Although I don't recall her exact words, I can remember how she made me feel. Perhaps it was because I was not often affirmed that the impact of her kind comment remained with me.

Attending St. John the Baptist broadened my horizons. I made a lot of new acquaintances and I explored the villages that surrounded the school. After school was dismissed in the evening, instead of going home, I would hang out with the older girls. We never seemed to be in a hurry to go home. The older girls had relatives in a village between the school and my village. Since they were visiting relatives they did not need an excuse for not going directly home after school. Husbands' plantation was between Halls Village where their relatives lived, and Cave Hill, my village. Often we would walk the long, lonely way home on Husbands' Road. This meant walking with cane fields on both sides. When the sugarcane was ripe and towering, it was as if you were entrapped. The absence of motor vehicle traffic caused the road to be desolate and scary, a very dangerous place for young girls to walk alone. It wasn't that I didn't have bus fare—I would spend the bus fare and walk with the others. Being with friends meant a lot to me. It gave me a sense of belonging.

In a sense my childhood experiences, particularly the absence of my mother, contributed to my early decision-making. As a result I was called 'hard-ears', meaning disobedient. As a result of this particular experience, I understand the importance of a loving, caring structure in a precocious child's life. The smarter the child is, the more important it is to have guidance from a caring guardian.

I transferred to St. John the Baptist shortly before it was time for me to take the 11-Plus exam. Not every student went to high school. When one took the 11-Plus exam, the score determined which high school you attended. The high-scoring children attended the top government schools such as Combermere, Harrison College, Queen's College and St. Michael's. Then there was Richmond, which was a trade school. By the time I sat for the exam, private high schools were becoming popular. Unlike the government schools, there was a cost. Nevertheless, parents were glad for the options these schools offered.

I was in the generation when more children, regardless of their social and economic status, were beginning to attend high school. In my mother's time only those with money, the right color, and the dark-skinned ones whose parents were married were privileged to attend high school. For many parents, sending a child to one of the private high schools was the ultimate sacrifice. Usually, the last grade in elementary school would be the end of the formal education. Much later, when secondary education became mandatory, the government opened many more high schools.

I did not do well on the 11-Plus test. As soon as you mentioned the word 'test' I became nervous. I also now understand that a child's emotional well-being contributes significantly to how well a child performs in school. Nevertheless, Ma decided to sacrifice and send me to a little-known school named The Malvern Academy. I attended Malvern Academy, which at the time was located on Hindsbury Road in St. Michael. I don't remember learning anything there. I remember one of my teachers, because he had the same last name as me. I also remember a few of the students, particularly the girl who beat me up because I was not a fighter. Although I remember the fight, I don't remember what it was about.

At this time Ma's live-in domestic job was conveniently located on my route to school. This enabled me to visit Ma in the morning and sometimes in the evening. After the morning visit, I walked the two plus miles to school. In the evening I would retrace my steps. I only visited in the servant room. I got the feeling that I didn't belong, as if I had to be hidden when

I stopped in. This was such a crucial time in my development. I wanted so much to belong. Ma certainly did her best, but her best was not satisfying my deep need to belong.

One of the girls in my class lived almost on the road to school. I started diverting to her house so I could walk with her to school. Soon I felt she didn't want me there. Again, I felt the pangs of rejection. The time came when I was no longer allowed to visit Ma after school. What a difference it would have made if during my adolescence I was made welcome where my mother spent most of her time. I was not, therefore after school I walked miles to the city and took the bus home to an empty house. This was when I started visiting my father's family. When Ma found out, she was very unhappy. She believed that I was not going to school and she never wanted me to get familiar with my father's family. The reality was, I went to school more often than not. My grades also reflected my state of being at the time. It wasn't that I didn't want to learn. It wasn't that I didn't want to go to school. It was that I was a lost girl not getting the love and attention from those close to me. Eventually Ma decided to stop wasting her money and at the age of twelve, she pulled me out of school.

By the time I got to the Malvern Academy I was a traumatized adolescent. In addition to not doing well academically, I was beginning to have behavioral issues. Ma was at her wit's end. Since I had now connected with my father's family, she was convinced that what she feared the most had become a reality. She was witnessing her daughter becoming like her undesirable father and his family. I only met one of my father's brothers and he was a hard-working carpenter. His oldest sister was deeply religious and austere. His other three sisters smoked and drank when that was rare for a woman in Barbados.

I was only eleven when I started high school, but I had experienced a lot. Hence I was quite old in my understanding. Since I was left on my own a lot I grew up very fast. In addition to the rape at the age of eight, I was molested at eleven, the summer before I entered high school. Remember the vulnerable route across the hill, sometimes among cane fields, that I took to Mrs. Hinkson's house? Well, one day I was followed by a St. Lucian man name Francis.

He was one of the young men who worked at the cement factory across from Papa's house. This incident had far reaching consequences and I was once again made to feel like I was the worst person in the world. Francis did not only molest me, he gave me a sexual disease, for which I had to seek medical help. This added to my feeling of unworthiness.

Ma was truly concerned for my health. She thought that I would become sterile as a result. Her profound faith prompted her to write and request prayer for me from Oral Roberts, an American Evangelist and founder of Oral Roberts University, seeking prayers for me. In addition to answering Ma's requests, he sent her a prayer cloth that I had to pin to my underwear. I do not recall how long I attended the clinic, but I was healed. During this time because I was at puberty, my perspiration was very strong. Instead of being lovingly guided in how to take care of myself, I heard negative derogatory comments that made me feel like I was making my perspiration strong. I am now aware of how young and uninformed my caregivers were.

THREE

The Madness of Youth

For children LOVE is spelt TIME.
- Zig Ziglar -

Children's behavior reflect the consciousness or the
unconsciousness of their ancestors.

I CAN still remember Ms. Field pleading with my mother to not take me out of school. Ms. Field was from one of the old families in the village and she was always at home. According to my mother, it was her sister Ms. Rita who named me Viterose. I suppose Ms. Field, being much older, knew that an idle preteen girl spelled trouble. As I reflect back, this was an opportunity for her to mentor a child without a father and almost without a mother. However, since we live in a world where we feel responsibility only toward our own, she felt no responsibility toward me. In fact, she never even offered me a cup of water. At that time in my life all I wanted was for someone to care enough to give me loving guidance. Children are like dogs: they take love from whoever offers it. Thus begun the most vulnerable period of my life.

With very little to do and nowhere to go, I found things to do, most often innocent, but as I grew older, not so innocent. I did have a few chores like bringing water and making sure the sheep were fed and watered. Many homes in Barbados at that time did not have water. There were public pipes located on public roads in the villages. Most homes had large drums that were kept filled for daily purposes. I brought many heavy buckets of water on my head. It was during this period that I developed the habit of doing everything fast. I found that when I brought the water quickly, I was praised. That gave me a good feeling, for I generally got very little positive encouragement.

I don't know the reason, but at this time I was no longer going to Papa's house. Daily I hung out in the street or at someone's house. I would visit anyone who would have me. I spent a lot of time talking to Ms. Field, but rarely did I go into her house. She would open her window and talk to me, or I would sit in her doorway. I remember one day these decent-looking people came looking for my mother. They came to Ms. Field's house and asked where my mother lived. I was there, but I was up in the plum tree. I came down to greet them after they found out I was my mother's daughter. I remember it as though it was yesterday, how I felt in their presence. I became very aware that I was an unkempt sight. My clothes were dirty and I am sure my hair needed combing.

Such was my existence. They happened to be relatives of Ma's uncle on her mother's side. They were bringing the Christmas money he sent every year since their mother's death. He already had a negative feeling about who his sister married and I certainly was not a good representation. He lived in America and I suppose since his family was coming to visit, he sent them to deliver the money.

In addition to Ms. Field, I hung out at another neighbor's house. Mrs. Firth was a newlywed and a newcomer to Cave Hill. What drew me and others to her house was the water in her yard. She was one of the few people who had the convenience of water. However, when the pipes* in our village, including hers, were off as would sometimes happen, I would go to a village farther away and bring water from the public pipe for her. Some days the only food I ate was what Mrs. Firth gave me. Even though Ma did provide something for me, hers was hot and delicious. Another reason why the young girls in the community gravitated to her house was because her very handsome brothers often visited. I thought the tall, brown-skinned one who shared the same birthday as me was cute, but at that time I was too young. Fifty years later, after his wife's death and I was then divorced, we reconnected. However, one of his daughters thought her dead mother was the only love he needed, so that ended a promising relationship.

There was a joiner's shop in the same community. Sometimes I visited the shop to talk to the owner. He was a much older man. The truth is, although I was sexually abused as a child, I was still naive. He was never inappropriate with me, we just talked. However, one day while we were talking a young woman from the community came. I did not have the understanding then that she probably saw me as a challenge to whatever was going on between them. I cannot tell you what started a confrontation between her and me, but I do know that I picked up one of his screwdrivers and stabbed her. Certainly, the police were called and I was taken to the police station.

My mother had to leave her job and come to the police station, which was not very far from her workplace. I was released to Ma with the condition that we would make an appointment with the probation officer. Ms. Weeks was the probation officer. She quickly summed up my situation and did not comply with my mother's wishes. Ma desperately wanted me sent to Dodds, or the girls' equivalent to Dodds— Dodds was the jail for teenaged boys. I know that Ms. Weeks realized that I was a child who needed loving guidance and attention. She tried to place me in a home, but it never materialized. Looking back, I can understand my mother's frustration. She had to work to support us. Her absence was of necessity and not of choice. I was placed on probation for one year and I never got into that kind of trouble again. The truth is, stabbing someone was not my nature. The universe knows, I was beaten up many times because I was not a fighter.

During the period of my life between twelve and fourteen I was like a ship without a rudder. Eventually Ma, with Ms. Field's persuasion, sent me to be a needlework apprentice. I joined the two other girls who were already there. Both were at least two years older than I. My apprenticeship quickly ended when I was accused of gossiping about the seamstress, who was a very young, married woman. It was not possible for me to talk about her indiscretions because I was not aware of them. Yes, I was present, but I was naive and not yet cognizant of such behavior. Nevertheless, someone requested that the radio station play the ballad *You Talk Too Much* for me. Another evidence of my low sense of self and insecurity was that I talked a lot. However, in this instance, I couldn't repeat what I was unaware of.

I know what vulnerability feels like. I knew as a child how it felt to be blamed and accused of situations and acts that I was not guilty of. I also knew what it felt like not to have anyone believe in me. My mother died when I was 62. I don't think she ever believed in me. Although the apprenticeship was short-lived, it did awaken within me a natural talent. Much later I would become an amazing tailor, just another one of my natural talents.

Of course, as a developing teen, it did not take long for me to become a target of the male species. I did not even know I was good-looking. Montgomery Boys' School was located in front of Mrs. Hinkson's house. While school was in session I sometimes got water from the pipe outside the school. I also had to pass by the school to get to Ms. Field's house. I was like a magnet drawing any attention I could get. I even drew the attention of a few male teachers. One in particular was middle-aged Mr. Good, who befriended me. He was a mulatto and according to Bajans, he was from a 'good family'. More than likely that meant he was from the planter class. One Saturday he invited me to his house. What I did not know was that his wife was a Seventh-Day Adventist. This meant she went to church on Saturdays. This particular Saturday she did not go to church. I am grateful that she didn't, because I later found out that he had a penchant for luring young girls.

A year or so after Ma took me out of school I became very promiscuous. I was not looking for sex. I was looking for love and acceptance, and the men were always ready to satisfy their needs with any vulnerable, naive girl child. Barbados was a very religious society, and sex was the worst sin, particularly pre-marital sex. The hypocrisy of this was startling. As mentioned earlier, the larger percentage of babies were born out of wedlock, and often church women had to get married because they became pregnant. Then they in turn would put out their pregnant teenaged daughters because the church did not condone such sin.

No one had a good word to say about me during that time in my life. I later looked back at that time and realized that no Christ-like love was extended to me. Instead I was told I would never amount to anything, and I was evil. Ironically, boys and men kept their reputations regardless of how they acted sexually. In fact, males were never considered promiscuous, only females. Consequently, my feeling of self-worth was further compounded by voluntary and involuntary sex. I was often taken advantage of, but I had no one to turn to. As a result of my terrible teen years, I have great compassion for young people. I feel I understand their pain. I mostly know that if adults honored the spirits of children from birth, their teen years would be less problematic.

Ma got married when I was thirteen years old. After she got married she worked as a grocery store clerk and was able to come home every night. I was jealous of this relationship, for I saw her giving him the attention which I never received. I believe my mother loved me in her own way, but when I was a troubled teen looking for love, she never showed me any. She would pass me on the street and act like she didn't know me. She would talk down at me, never to me. I understood this and I would tell her to talk to me, not at me. Of course, in telling her this I was being rude. Even then I understood my emotional needs, but was incapable of verbalizing them. Who wanted to listen to me anyhow? Like many mothers, she would not believe me when I had reason to complain about her husband. Thank goodness, my reputation was worse than my actions.

Eventually my behavior and the stress of Ma's

life was too much and she too succumbed to tuberculosis. I was the one who made her ill, so more guilt was piled on. I was thirteen when she got married and she was home when I became pregnant at fourteen. This meant that shortly after she was married she was hospitalized for six months. Again I felt as if I was all alone. Can you imagine the vulnerability? One of Ma's Christian friends in the village provided me with one meal a day when Ma was gone. This same lady became my baby's godmother. Since she fed me, I hung out at her house. Once again, in spite of what my reputation was, I was successful at staving off the Christian wolf she was married to.

If indeed sex was my intent, there were so many men I could have slept with. My true intent was to feel loved and secure. Eventually, or so I thought, I developed a relationship with a young man who became my baby's father. This young man was about seven years older. His family lived close to Papa's house. He had eleven siblings and I was familiar with the older siblings. In fact, it was one of his sisters I hung out with when I attended St. John the Baptist Girls' School. I would see him, his brothers and father quarrying stone as I travelled on the lonely path over the hill to Mrs. Hinkson's house. Sometimes when I passed he and one of his brothers would call out to me "come to me white lamb and eat from my hand." I then ran away from them as fast as I could. A little older now and with no supervision, at night I often hung out in the streets with whomever was hanging out around the churches or in the streets. I was not the only girl doing this. This 'hanging out' resulted in many babies being born.

At first he seemed to really care. Instead of hanging with the crowd we would hang out together. He was tall, dark and handsome, but with an awful temper. A temper, he told me many years later, that he modified after thinking about the example he needed to set for his children. I am not sure how long the courtship lasted, but it ended soon after I became pregnant. He even disowned the baby, which is typical of young, irresponsible men. Additionally, I suppose because I was under-age, he was afraid of getting into trouble with the law. Funny thing is, I most recently, after fifty years, met up with the woman that became pregnant for him shortly after me and I discovered that I am a few months older then she is. The difference was, her mother embraced him. Although coming from a large family, he too was looking for love and acceptance. My mother treated him with scorn and disdain. She knew I was too young, and he was not who she would've chosen for me. Therefore there was no encouragement for the relationship. He was not even allowed at our house.

Eleven months after my daughter was born, the other girl gave birth to a daughter. She bore two more children for him. Forty-five years later I reached out to their youngest son who is now serving time in a US jail for murder. From him I learned that the relationship which I was so jealous of and I believed was so great, really was not. She eventually left him and married someone else. After my baby was born resembling his family, he supported the baby, but he stopped as soon as I got married. I also found out from his son in jail that he did the same to them after their mother left him.

Today my daughter, the stone that the builder rejected, is the only one of his four children that he communicates with. I believe that this is so because I never painted a negative picture of him to her. Furthermore she was never truly embraced by the man I married, even though he adopted her. When she graduated from high school and went back to Barbados for a visit, she reached out to her father and he responded positively. He still resides in Barbados, but they call each other for birthdays and holidays.

I caught a 'nine-month cold'. That is what my mother's shopkeeper told her when referring to my pregnancy. Teen pregnancy ages you very quickly, particularly when you are abandoned by the people who are supposed to care for you. I was put out in the streets with nowhere to go and no means of support. Hence, I was at anyone's mercy. I found my way to my aunt's house—my father's sister. It was there that I met a young man who eventually took me to his mother's house and where I lived and ate until the baby was born. These people did not know me, but yet they were kind to me. I cannot remember how much medical attention I received during the pregnancy, but the baby was delivered in the only maternity clinic in Barbados at the time. A few weeks before I delivered I ran into my mother in Bridgetown and we spoke. What I did not know is that the boyfriend of the woman I was living with had found his way to my mother's house and had given her a blow by blow account of my daily activity. When I did deliver, Ma came to the maternity ward and took me and the baby to her house.

I was now a child with a child, with no means of support except what little the baby's father brought. I was totally dependent upon my mother for all my needs. There was no social welfare in Barbados. Things went well at Ma's house for a while as long as I did what I was told. Eventually, Ma asked me to leave again and I ended up living with the baby's aunt. However, the stress and lack of proper nutrition became too much, and I too contracted tuberculosis. In fact, my mother noticed that I was looking sick and took me back home. I was sent to the clinic and from there I went to the hospital. The only reason I was sent to the hospital for six weeks was because the baby was too young to be further exposed to TB. Further compounding my low self-esteem was the stigma associated with having TB.

Amazingly, out of what may appear to be

awful, sometimes is a catalyst for good. It was while I was in the hospital that my uncle came home from London for a vacation. He was also at that time looking for a wife. He found her right there on the TB ward at the Queen Elizabeth Hospital. My uncle is tall, dark and handsome like his father. He is also very sensitive. Hence when he came to visit me in the hospital, he cried. The nurse on duty that day found him attractive, and they somehow connected. Eventually she followed him to England where they were married and lived for many years. They eventually migrated to Canada where their two children were born and she died in 2008. Their migration to Canada in the early seventies coincided with my family's migration to the US. Hence we sometimes visited each other.

After the six-month stay in the hospital, I returned home. I had to find work to help support myself. Perhaps it was an advertisement on the only radio station in Barbados that informed me about the company that was looking for women to smock girls' clothes. It was an American company that brought the Polly Flinders dress parts to Barbados and many of us smocked them for very low wages. I was glad to have a means of supporting myself.

Having a regular wage enabled me to buy fabric from the 'coolie man'?*. These East Indian men we called 'coolie men' contributed significantly to the economic development of Barbados. They travelled throughout the villages trusting their wares to all who consented to pay weekly what they could afford. Sometimes that was as little as fifty cents. They had great patience, for often after taking their goods, week after week some women would hide from them. They made fabric available for clothes and curtains, and they also sold small household utensils. Readymade clothes were unheard of in my circles, therefore all women had dressmakers and men had tailors.

I did smocking for a number of years. During this period of time I was living at home and being a good girl. I remember commending myself for being celibate for more than two years. My feelings were that I would show them that I was not as bad as they thought. We picked up our smocking and delivered it at buildings close to the Garrison Savannah. I met my future husband on the bus one night when I was returning from the dressmaker. Thereafter he would pick me up at the Garrison after I dropped off my work. I was only seventeen years old, but I was all grown up. Still looking for love and acceptance, I would eventually become pregnant and be forced to marry.

FOUR

Married Life

There is so much bad in the best of us and
so much good in the worst of us,
that it behooves none of us to
talk about the rest of us.

- Robert Louis Stevenson -

IRONICALLY, THE man I married was a member of the Seventh Day Adventist church; not just a member, but an elder in the church. I, a rotten apple, seduced this very upright man who was ten years my senior. I became pregnant again and as the practice went, I was forced to get married. Of course, if he had listened to anyone in the village, he never would have married me. As a result of his indiscretion he lost his job as a seller of adventist books, and was dismembered from the church for a period of time. After we got married I moved into his mother's house and lived with his mother and two sisters. It was then that I began my illusory life—illusory in the sense that I was wearing my Christian mask of righteousness. It was important that what I believed to be my sordid past had to be kept hidden. How naïve I was. I even considered insisting on being called by my first name instead of my second name. I was feeling that the name I was known by was tarnished. Truthfully, anything done in our universe cannot be hidden. Even though it may take years to be revealed, it eventually surfaces.

The marriage was an opportunity to prove that I was not all bad. It also gave me a feeling of belonging. I determined in my mind that I was going to show the tongue waggers that there was good in me. Boy, did I have to prove myself! What did I know about marriage at seventeen? Absolutely nothing. I did not even know what love was. I had never experienced it. All I knew was that I was married to a man years older, and hence I had the father figure and the security I always wanted. How wrong I was. I also now understand that we attract into our lives what we are, not what we want. I was looking for love, acceptance and intimacy, but I didn't get what I was incapable of giving. I quickly learned that even to ask for a loaf of bread engendered a quarrel. It seemed that I could not do or say anything that was right. My very insecure self felt like it was living in a sea of self-righteousness. After all, I was the awful sinner. I much later found out that in the beginning my husband even went to my mother with his opinion about our disagreements, and not having a good opinion about me, she believed the worst. The obvious self-righteousness caused me to embrace the quotation at the beginning of this chapter. It brought me hope, and thus it became my mantra.

All my soul was longing for was someone to believe in me and love me. Contributing to the conflict in the early days of the marriage was my lack of compliance with the rules and regulations of the church. However, one night I dreamt that the end of the world had come and I was lost. Consequently, I joined the church. I became a member of a 'chosen few'. I did so with great fervor and diligence.

In the meantime I relentlessly dedicated

myself to the role of being a good wife, even though from the beginning I felt I had made a mistake. I know now that there are no mistakes in life, just lessons to be learned. Living with my in-laws was a cultural shock. Although from the same country, their way of living was so different from what I was used to. Being a born leader, I spearheaded as many changes as I could. Getting to know my husband caused me to realize, even then, that if I had grown up he would not have been my choice for a husband. The funny thing is, everyone thought I was so lucky to get such a good husband, but my experience caused me to think differently. I definitely did not get a loving, caring husband. What I later came to understand was that as a result of his childhood, he too had unresolved pain and great insecurity. It took me many years to sort out that I was not solely to be blame for the issues of our marriage. We both had deep psychological issues that needed resolving. Compounding our issues was the Christian dogma that the man is the head of the home. As Pastor Coon, the Adventist minister, stated: "even if he put his dirty socks in the frying pan the woman must not say anything."

Though troubled and very young, I had the uncanny ability to get things done. I had a can-do-it attitude. Therefore 'following a parked car' was not easy for me. My husband wanted a wife that followed for the sake of following, I was not that woman. I am not the type that agrees just because a man says it is square I have to agree it is square. This was the kind of wife my husband wanted. As a result, he never respected that what I brought to the table was what was needed.

I possessed a strength that took advantage of every opportunity that came my way. My strength and this character trait created marital problems. The dogma of what role a man must have in a marriage caused me to be dissatisfied with my husband because he did not have a strong take-charge personality. Since I didn't grow up with any male role models, my idea of what and how a man was to act was limited. I started very early in the marriage to lose respect for him. Of course, not coming from a secure childhood, it is understandable that a sense of security was on the top of my list of needs.

The baby was born while we were still living in my in-laws' house. We called her Catherine with a C, because Queen Elizabeth visited Barbados around the time she was born and we wanted to name her after someone in the royal family, alive or deceased. She was a beautiful, healthy baby, with a head full of the coarsest hair a baby ever had. She was much loved by the in-laws because she was the first grandchild. As much as she was loved, her crying at night became problematic. So we moved. This time we moved to my husband's aunt's house in another village within walking distance. His aunt and her husband were in England and only his grandmother stayed in their house. The house had three bedrooms, therefore there was plenty of room for us. My oldest daughter who lived with my mother visited on weekends.

I became the woman of the house and I took my responsibilities seriously. I kept the house and the surrounding yard clean and tidy. Keeping the yard clean was significant, for there were chickens sleeping in the trees and what a mess they made. As young as I was, my cooking was the best. For some reason I always knew how to cook well, even though no one taught me how to cook. In fact, from a very early age, everything I did, I did well. Living with my husband's grandmother was a good experience. She was a pleasant elderly lady. We shared our meals with her, otherwise she took care of herself. Our eldest son was born while we lived with grandmother. She and Erwin became best buddies. Unlike Catherine, Erwin was a good baby. He was so quiet that it took visitors a while to know a baby was in the house. Once his belly was full he was contented. Back then I was regimented. My babies were readily placed on feeding schedules. I would feed him and go to Bridgetown and know that he would sleep until I returned. I later learned that as he got older grandmother comforted him with her breast.

It was while living with grandmother that my mother's oldest brother came home from England for a visit with his wife and two children. We were told that he had brought a package and there was something in it for everyone. Therefore we all gathered at Papa's house the day the gifts were going to be handed out. To my dismay, there was nothing for me. Unquestionably I was disappointed, and believed it demonstrated that even he did not think too highly of me. By this time I was feeling a little better about myself. As a member of the Adventist church I held the belief of being 'better' or 'favored' because I went to church on Saturday. This gave me a sense of self that I had never experienced before, even though many years later I came to understand it was a false belief.

Since so few people expressed confidence in me, I clearly remember those who did. The head elder of the Adventist church we attended recognized my ability and expressed it. As a result I was given leadership roles in that particular church. I also credit the Adventist church for the start of my real education. In my soul there was a hunger for greater understanding, and through the Adventist Church I came to understand that reading was the key. Every Saturday, worldwide, the members of every Seventh Day Adventist Church study the same lesson in many different languages. In our Sabbath school class in Barbados, I wanted to make a meaningful contribution to the discussion. When I came to the realization that to do so I had to read, I began reading with a passion. I would read and reread with a dictionary handy. As an Adventist I found there were always lots of books. One was encouraged to study for oneself. Unfortunately, you were only encouraged to read and study literature written from an Adventist perspective, hence the process of brainwashing. There was one particular book, supposedly written by Ellen G. White, the prophet of the Adventist Church, titled Positive Christian Living. It is the only Adventist book I still own. Reading that book gave me the desire to live impeccably. It also lit the spark of possibility thinking that was within me because in this book she admonishes to shoot for the stars. As a result of the Adventism health message, to this day, although I am not an Adventist, I continue to eat healthily. Long before anyone else, Adventists taught the benefit of healthy eating. Unfortunately, adhering to the health message was made a mandate for being saved or going to heaven. In reality, not all Adventists adhered to the health message. Here again is another religious dogma, which was not a bad idea, yet the way it was presented contributed to man's dilemma because it created a sense of guilt when you ate what you preferred.

After the first stormy years of marriage we

settled into a comfortable routine. There was no great romance in the marriage, so I dutifully performed my role as a wife. In spite of that, I cannot say there was true intimacy. I think it was because neither of us knew how to create an intimate relationship.

My early marriage and my disturbing childhood did not nullify the burning desire I had within to excel. Mediocrity did not sit well with me. In Barbados at that time, having a baby out of wedlock was the end of most possibilities for a young woman. I was not content to settle. So when I heard on the radio that the YMCA was offering a handicraft course, I was willing and ready to attend. My only obstacle was my mother-in-law, who had to babysit. In her world, my place was at home. With perseverance I managed to attend a few cross-stitching classes, but my real opportunity came four years into the marriage.

FIVE

Emigration to America

(Upon man) God bestowed seeds
pregnant with all possibilities.

- Pico Mirandola -

MY BIG opportunity came when my aunt returned home from America for a visit. To most Barbadians, America was the land of milk and honey. A contributing factor to this belief was the migrant workers who, while working in America, sent home money and pretty things to their girlfriends and wives. Historically, men like Papa, my great-grandfather, capitalized on the economic opportunity America afforded in the early 1900s. They returned home to buy land and they usually had the biggest houses in the village. They could afford furnishings that the ordinary Barbadian could not afford. Furnishings like the player piano in the living room of Papa's house. In the 1960s men were still travelling to America as migrant workers, and it had become easier for women to find work as domestics and get sponsored.

My aunt readily agreed when I asked her to help me get to America. Shortly after she returned home, she sent a letter asking me to come for a visit. I took the letter to the American Embassy and was granted a three-month visa. All who were going to be affected by my absence, including my mother-in-law, saw it as an opportunity. Therefore arrangements were made for the children to be kept. Claudette continued to stay with my mother, and Catherine and Erwin stayed with their father and his family. Leaving my children behind was difficult, but I had no intention of leaving them longer than I had to. I was going to America to make a way for them.

My excitement at traveling to America was indescribable. My mother gave God all the praise for the way he was working in my life. To her he had taken the barren land, me, and turned it into a fertile field. To me it was another notch on the ladder as I reached for the stars. I was only twenty-one, a wife and a mother of three, with many regrets and a fervent desire to make the past invisible if that was possible. My affirmation for that period in my life was part of a scripture found in Philippians 3:13-14, *"forgetting what lies behind and straining forward to what lies ahead, I press on toward the goal for the prize of the upward call of God in Christ Jesus."*

My aunt and her family were only in America for a short time. Nevertheless she happily made it possible for me to emigrate and shortly thereafter my cousin Shirley followed. My aunt and her family were far from established when she helped us come to America, so I greatly appreciated her sacrifice and willingness to help us, even without her husband's approval.

I left Barbados for New York in November 1969. My port of entry was Kennedy Airport in Queens, New York. My first glimpse of America was disappointing, to be sure. I was not prepared to see such dilapidated buildings, streets full of pot holes and littered in trash. Neither was I prepared for the many homeless poor people, as I had expected to see evidence of prosperity everywhere. Despite my first impression, I had come to better my position, and we set out as soon as possible to get me started.

Although it was illegal for people to work while there on vacation, there was a thriving underground industry and my aunt was armed with the information. We went to an immigration lawyer who readily placed me with a Jewish family in New Jersey. Years later when the immigration people began cracking down on immigrants his law office was shut down, but not before he had made lots of money. He received compensation from the illegal workers and their employers. When the three months allotted on my visa expired, I applied for three more and they were granted, but I eventually stayed longer than I was legally allowed to.

At first I was perplexed by the seeming sameness of every street corner in Jamaica, New York. The many storefronts and fruit and vegetable stands all appeared the same to me and I was sure I would never find my way around. Much to my aunt's amazement though, in a short time I was negotiating the place as if I had lived there for a long time. I worked in New Jersey during the week and came home on Saturday afternoons. To get to the Laws' house in Livingston New Jersey, I took the bus from my aunt's house to the subway station. Then I took the subway to Port Authority, where I caught the Morristown, New Jersey bus, which after an hour or so got me to little town called Livingston. Then I walked a half a mile to the Laws' house.

There was much to see and learn. I relished the challenges and the opportunity to learn. I used my aunt's etiquette book to teach myself the correct way to set a table and other things I thought I would need to know while working in the white people's house. I was cognizant of my very broken Barbadian creole English, and I set out to speak the Queen's English. I succeeded, for years later while I was living in New Hampshire some of the members of the church were surprised that my formal education was limited. Succeeding at speaking properly did not take away the loathing I had for my strong voice. As I listened to refined female voices that I encountered, I thought my voice was not at all feminine. I am not sure when the loathing went away, but I am now quite comfortable with the strength of my voice.

The Laws family was a husband and wife

and three children, all girls. I was totally responsible for cleaning the entire house and doing all the laundry. I did not mind the work, because to this day I enjoy housework. I gain great satisfaction from seeing the results of my handiwork so readily. However, Mrs. Law's house had to be cleaned a particular way. I was expected to clean the three bathrooms, three bedrooms, kitchen, den and study every day. The fixtures in the bathroom had to be sparkling. The formal dining room and living room I cleaned every Friday, and I had to make sure there were never any fingerprints on the walls. When I vacuumed the living room and dining room, which had a beautiful wall to wall moss-colored green rug of the highest quality, I could not leave any footprints. In the beginning the hardest part of working for the Laws was the fact that I did not get to go to church. The wife insisted that I take care of the house before I left on Saturdays. Therefore my days off were Saturday afternoon to Monday morning.

This was a new experience for me, but because I knew how to clean it did not take me long to master the procedure. In the end I was the benefactor, for years later I would be trusted to clean when no one was home. I was always commended for leaving the homes spotlessly clean. The small price I paid was enduring the insults of Mrs. Law, who was not very kind. She made sure that I understood that she knew I did not come from anywhere and that I was not accustomed to anything. The irony was, I had what she would have given anything to have, and that was good health. Shortly after I was hired she died of cancer of the liver at the age of thirty. Perhaps I had the misfortune of encountering her when she was sick and this explains her meanness toward me.

After her death I became a very significant part of that household. At twenty-two I ran that house, doing everything except the food shopping. I continued to do the housework as usual. I became responsible for the girls in addition to sometimes preparing meals. I was in my element. I was in charge with no one looking over my shoulder and I prided myself in doing a good job. Mr. Law even marveled at my ability. He once said to me: "Elaine you don't work hard you are just efficient." He was a good, kind soul. However, although my work load increased, my pay remained the same:

seventy five dollars weekly.

For a short time after her daughter's death the wife's mother came every weekend and stayed for longer periods. It was from her I learned how to prepare the meals the way the family liked them. She eventually came less and less, and finally she stopped coming altogether. She would call, however, and wanted me to tell her what Mr. did and where he went. It was none of my business, so she never heard anything from me.

In the meantime, through the immigration lawyer, the Laws filed for my permanent residency and it was decided that I would stay in the country until the papers came through. The first part went through quickly. My application was accepted without a hitch and what remained was waiting for the call to go home and pick up my permanent residency papers. The whole process was completed in just under a year, which was amazingly rapid considering that many waited for years to get their papers.

The year away from my children was hard. It was difficult for the children also, but I never knew how taxing it truly was until I returned home. Catherine, in particular, cried all the way home from the airport. Many years later she accused me of abandoning her. However, the separation was another very important part of my development. I came to grips with my lack of feelings for my husband, but it was too late. I wrote home often, but there were never the kinds of letters a wife wrote to a husband she loved. He even complained to my mother. She wrote me about it, but it made no difference.

Even though I would faithfully play the role for twenty-four more years, I knew then without a doubt that if I had a choice I would not have married him. Who could I tell my feelings to? I was lucky to be married. What I found most problematic was his lack of responsibility when it came to providing for his family. He settled for so little. Adventism offered young men and women opportunity. After joining the Adventist church, many went to the Adventist College in Trinidad and studied for a profession or learned a trade. He would talk about it, but never followed through.

I returned to Barbados in 1970. By the time I got there my husband had rented a house in the same gap (many short streets in Barbados are called gaps) as his aunt's house. It was also located five minutes from the Caribbean sea. Being so close to the ocean meant we went for many early morning dips. I never learned to swim, but he was a fish. We went very early because the water felt warmer before the sun came up.

The money I saved while in America gave us the ability to buy furniture and the fridge I always envisioned having, on credit. I fell back into the routine of being a wife and mother. My children were my world and I resolved to be the virtuous woman of Proverbs 31. I cooked and sewed and had sex and played the part well. We never had a lot of money, but the rent was paid and there was always enough to eat. Although not satisfied, I was content. Maybe my contentment was based on the knowledge that shortly I would be immigrating to America permanently.

In addition to getting furniture from the money I saved, I was also able to fix my teeth. In recent years, one of my dentists in America marveled at the quality of the few teeth I have left. I began losing my teeth at an early age. Often when I went to work with Mrs. Hinkson it was because I was going to the hospital to get my teeth pulled. My smile was reserved when I traveled to America in 1969, but when I returned in 1971, I had a beautiful smile. For years, losing my teeth at such an early age was a source of embarrassment for me. I never wanted anyone to know that I wore dentures. I was blessed because the first dentures I got looked so good that people who knew me never knew I wore dentures unless I told them. I turned my misfortune into my children's opportunity. They all have beautiful teeth because I made sure that their teeth were cared for. My effort to get them to the dentist at least once a year was often met with opposition, but nothing or no one was going to get in the way of my children's dental care.

When I returned to America one year later, Mr. Law was glad to have me back. I resumed my trek to Livingston and assumed my responsibilities. By this time Mr. Law was diligently looking for a wife. He eventually found one whose husband had been killed by a drunken driver on the New Jersey Turnpike, leaving her with three children, two boys and a girl. They soon got married and became the Laws bunch, after The Brady Bunch on television with their six children. Six children necessitated more room. Therefore we moved to a bigger house in another part of New Jersey, which I believe was closer to his work in Newark. There was now a lot more house to clean and double the amount of laundry, but my new mistress was easier to work for. She never gave me orders. Since she knew I knew what I was doing, she allowed me to continue taking care of the house as usual. Her youngest was just a toddler so I helped with his care and also helped with the preparation of meals. It was much easier working for her. To this day, I think of those children and wonder what they are like as men and women.

My working hours changed when I returned. I was now able to leave on Friday evenings, allowing me to go to church on Saturdays. This became the highlight of my week. I had visited the Seventh Day Adventist Church in Jamaica, New York when I first arrived because the wife of my aunt's landlord was a Seventh Day Adventist. The majority of the congregation were people from various Caribbean countries. Now free to attend church, it would become my church home. At first I felt all alone when I attended the church. Perhaps it was as a result of my feelings of insecurity and unworthiness. I would never forget the trip I took with the church to Atlantic City, for the Adventist big yearly conference. There were thousands of people there from all over the world. I even ran into some people I knew from Barbados, yet I felt so isolated.

My association with some of the Adventist elite at the church in New York made me aware of how coming to America, to some extent, leveled out the playing field when it came to quality of living. In New York all of us were aliens, living in the same kinds of housing and many times working illegally. In Barbados, as in the Caribbean region in general, this was not the case. The color of your skin, the size of the house, the amenities in your home, and your education placed you on a different stratum of society. This was even noticeable in the church in Barbados. In America, however, everyone lived in the same kind of apartment, had the same amenities and had to make the same scramble to find work and go through the same procedure to become residents. Hence, we became equal.

In time, I made friends. My first friend was a Jamaican who, like myself, was paving the way for his family to come to America. I met Walter at one of the many tent meetings the church held regularly simply to proselytize. On Saturday evenings we would hang out together. He had a single friend who had a car and often we would go to Brooklyn to visit some of their friends. Brooklyn was and is the Caribbean people's haven. I even became friends with Winston's sister and brother-in-law who lived close to my aunt's house. By this time my aunt and her husband had bought a house in Jamaica, Queens. My aunt had concerns about my association with these two men and I would be lying if I said they did not try to be more than just friends. They would not have been normal men if they did not, but our relationship was totally platonic. I had a long time before pledged to never be unfaithful to my marriage vows and I was able to live true to that pledge.

As time went by I made more friends and acquaintances at church. Two in particular, a young lady named Daphne, who is from the former British Honduras, now the country called Belize, and a childhood acquaintance named Lorraine. The three of us became best friends. Lorraine I knew when I went to Edgehill Girls' School. She had lived in the Wanstead Plantation big house because her stepfather owned Wanstead Plantation. Therefore she was not considered to be on my level. However she was so glad to see me and she reminded me of the kindness I expressed toward her in elementary school. She had once had a troublesome patch of ringworm on her leg. She said I always stood up for her when some of the children picked on her because of the infection. Her mother eventually took her out of Edgehill and I had not seen here for eighteen years or more.

My association with my first two male friends became a thing of the past, as Daphne, Lorraine and I looked forward to spending Saturdays together. We would go to Daphne's house for lunch and then lounge away the afternoon talking. Sometimes we went to the evening service. Of course our conversations were of a spiritual nature, because you could only talk about certain things on Sabbath. A sincere sisterhood had developed among the three of us. We remained friends even after my family came and we set up house. I saw more of Lorraine, for she came to our house almost every Saturday while she was in nursing school. The year we lived in New York, our home was her retreat. Lorraine eventually became the godmother to my youngest son. After we moved to New Hampshire, both she and Daphne visited us on more than one occasion.

Although my life has taken a different route to theirs, we still consider ourselves good friends. Many years have gone by since those days in New York—the days when we talked about everything. Although I was not much older, they looked to me for advice. Both of them got married and set up homes of their own. Their children are all grown now. Daphne has three children, Lorraine has one son. They are still staunch Seventh Day Adventists. I not only left the church, but I got a divorced, putting me in a totally different category. I visited Daphne in 2013 in Alabama after not seeing her for twenty-five years. She and her family were really quite glad to see me. She prepared a great feast to welcome me and my friend to her home. She and her husband are now proud grandparents of three. Lorraine, on the other hand, lives close to my graduate school friend in New York. So every time I visit that friend, I see Lorraine.

SIX

Our Life in New York

Family life is full of major and minor crises-
the ups and downs of health,
success and failure in career, marriage, and divorce-
and all kinds of characters.
It is tied to places and events and histories.

- Thomas Moore -

WHEN WOMEN emigrate seeking a better way of life for their children, the very act of leaving them behind fosters thoughts of abandonment in the children's minds. Since I was aware of this fact, I was determined that I was not going to leave my children in Barbados any longer than I had too. Shortly after I returned to America, I filed the necessary papers for my family to join me and in the meantime. I worked and saved my money. My salary increased to $95 per week and my boss began paying social security insurance for me. It was not a lot of money, but not having to buy food or contribute to living expenses, I was able to save most of it. After my boss got married and we moved to the new house, my days off were Friday and Saturday. Having Fridays off afforded me the opportunity to make a little more money. Therefore, every Friday, I gladly cleaned the house of the doctor my cousin Shirley worked for. I worked that second job until my husband arrived.

More help came in my preparation to set up house when my boss sold his house that had become too small for his bigger family. I received most of the household items such as pots, pans, kitchen utensils, curtains, bedspreads and bed linen. The only thing I paid for was the expensive solid oak master bedroom furniture. I was able to set up my first apartment with a lot more than I could have imagined. Acquiring the stuff was easy, but how was I going to get it from New Jersey to Queens, New York? At the time it seemed so far away. Eventually my aunt's husband rented a truck, drove to New Jersey to pick up my stuff, and stored it in their basement for as long as I needed it kept.

In less than a year the immigration paperwork was found satisfactory and my husband and children got their permanent visas. It was agreed that he would come first, find a job, and the two of us would get things ready for the children. I was very apprehensive at the thought of my husband coming to America, as by this time I had formed an unpleasant picture of his working ability. I understood the kind of hustle that was required to succeed in America, and I was not so sure that he had what it took.

After I returned to America, I racked my brain thinking of what he would do for work when he finally came. I thought that without a college education very few options were open to him. Compounding the situation was the fact that he could not work on Saturday, because it was the Sabbath. During the six years we were married, he had driven a bread truck for the first year, worked as a book salesman for the church, and in 1970, after I returned home, his limited income from book sales forced him to take a job as an insurance salesman. He liked this kind of work because he could work at his own pace, sleep when he wanted to and work when he wanted to. Of course, transitioning to America would not immediately offer him the kinds of options he had in Barbados.

He came to America in March of 1972. Being a member of the Adventist church proved to be extremely helpful during this transitional period. There were many women in the church who had followed the same route I was taking and knew the ropes. Hence there was an abundance of information about getting acclimated to the working world as a Caribbean immigrant woman. I was advised to register with the Adventist Agency in Brooklyn where they specialized in home health care. When the time came for me to say goodbye to the family in New Jersey, I had already registered and taken the training to become a home health aide. The three months before the children came, I worked as many jobs as I could. In the meantime things were more difficult for my husband. His lack of skills and his Sabbath keeping posed problems. Finally, after going to an agency every day for six weeks, he found a job working at a paint factory from 10 pm to 6 am.

When it came to housing, the Adventist

community again proved helpful. We rented a room from a member of Jamaica Church for the three months before the children came. In New York, the hustle of many Caribbean people was buying and renting as many homes as they could. They even rented rooms in the house they lived in. We benefited from this each time we needed a place. Since the children were coming we needed more than a room.

I had befriended a young Jamaican woman who belonged to Linden Boulevard Adventist church and lived on the same block as my aunt. As providence would have it, she and her husband bought another house in the suburbs, so their moving coincided with our need. Therefore we rented their two bedroom, downstairs apartment in an attached house. We were fortunate in this transitional period to have the support of my aunt and her family, and also the greater Adventist community. Much can be said for the value of being a part of an organization, particularly a worldwide one. We had a built-in network in the Adventist church. I don't think I recognized the value of it then, but looking back, I now realize the tremendous value of the support and guidance that were available to us at the time.

It was not my husband's idea to bring the children as quickly as I wanted them to come. He wanted to leave them home while we established ourselves economically. That was the norm. The majority of Caribbean people who immigrated to America or England usually left their children behind while they worked and provided material things. I thought differently. I told him if we were going to suck salt we were going to do it with the children. I knew of too many instances where the parents left the children home with relatives, sometimes even with friends. Although the parents worked and supported the children by sending money and parcels, when they did become united, the parents were strangers to their children. Although I knew that the children's grandparents would do the best they could for the children, I also knew from experience that no one cares for children like a mother.

I had already left them too long. Furthermore, it was for my children that I existed. They arrived in July of 1972. I was extremely happy to be united with them. Claudette was eight, Catherine was six and Erwin was four. I will never forget the evening my aunt's husband took us to the airport to get them. It was the end of our separation and the beginning of a long journey. That evening the gulf between my husband and Claudette was very noticeable—a gulf that has never been bridged. Children don't build relationships with adults, adults build relationships with children. It was obvious that there was no relationship between the two of them. I don't think he meant any malice, he simply did not know how.

We had the remainder of the summer to get reacquainted. They went wherever I went. I would never forget being so embarrassed by their 'rank' Barbadian broken English. Like the day I took them to the bank on Linden Boulevard and they began to talk. I could not wait to get them out of the bank. It didn't take them long, however, to drop the dialect. Unlike me, they have no trace of an accent. In the fall Claudette and Catherine were registered in Linden Seventh Day Adventist School. We were grateful that they wore uniforms because it was easier, and they were used to wearing uniforms in Barbados. Erwin was not old enough to go to school, so he became my working buddy.

He was very quiet and well behaved. Hence, he would go to the seniors' homes with me. While I worked he watched TV, or they would sometimes entertain him. One payday we went to the bank on Jamaica Avenue. It was particularly crowded that day and when we became separated, I was frantic. After I was unable to find him, I went to the nearest police station, and there he was happily eating a pastry the police had given him. I was never so happy to see anyone. He had wandered away from my side and I got lost in the crowd. That was a period of bonding for Erwin and me. I would often sing to him *my son, my son, you're everything to me…* We became really close.

We lived on a block that was at one time occupied by all-white families. As the blacks moved in the whites moved further out on Long Island. When we moved there, there were very few whites left, but we happened to live next door to one. My children were accustomed to the joy of play. In Barbados they were able to run and jump and skip like lambs. Living in the confinement of New York was unbearable for them. Sometimes we allowed them to run around the few feet of yard that was next to the house. To us it was unbelievable that the neighbors would find innocent children at play a problem. It became apparent to us that New York was not the place to raise children. Furthermore, Catherine had a continuous cough and low grade temperature, which the doctor diagnosed as bronchitis, which disappeared when we left New York.

Economically, life was tough. My husband had switched to a day job and I worked as much as I could. Our income was just enough to pay the rent, the utilities and buy food. We could not even afford to go to the laundermat. So every Sunday we hand-washed all the clothes and hung them in the basement to dry. Washing clothes by hand is what I did in Barbados, so this was not new. All my life I had to survive with very little. Consequently, I learned how to 'cut and contrive', as the Barbadians would say. In other words, I knew how to stretch a dollar.

In time I became dissatisfied with the situation as it was. In my frame of mind at the time, it appeared hopeless. Of course, I was of the opinion that the role of every good Christian man who was the head of his household was to be the breadwinner. I had no problem helping.

The keyword here is helping. I learned really fast that my husband had a comfort zone and regardless of how much we did without, he was not about to leave it. I must admit that as a result, I became quite resentful. To make matters worse, shortly after the children came I discovered I was pregnant. The thought of bringing another child into an already burdened situation, to me, was not an option. Therefore, with my husband's approval, I did what was available to me. I got an abortion.

We were surrounded by many Caribbean people who were working hard and capitalizing on the opportunities America offered. This was particularly true of Jamaicans. Many of the church members owned more than one house. Both the women and men worked more than one job to enable them to attain their American dream. My landlords were a classic example. Besides the house we lived in, which had renters in both apartments, the house they moved to on the island had renters on the second floor and in the basement. They lived on the first floor. I can still remember my landlady saying to me, "in twenty years these houses will be paid for and we will then be well off." Unfortunately, her marriage did not last the twenty years. Such was the mindset of the Caribbean people in New York.

I had that desire and I understood the push that was necessary to get ahead. However, I was not willing to sacrifice the well-being of my children. I looked toward my husband for possibilities and I saw none. I truly felt trapped. I would never forget the Sabbath when one of the elders at Jamaica Church said "being married to someone you don't love is like being in prison." His words rang true for me. Indeed I felt like I was confined with no way out. The result was tremendous guilt for many years. Many a Sunday, as I was in the basement doing the laundry, I would cry out to God to give me the love I needed for my husband. America had given us a chance to better ourselves. The two alternate years I was in America alone, had given me a taste of freedom and autonomy. My belief of the sky being the limit had gained scope with the possibilities available in America.

After my husband came I felt constrained. My thoughts and ideas were mostly met with opposition and reasons why there were not possible. As a result, I was often accused of wanting to, or trying to wear the pants. I was even told my mind was 'too high'. The situation never changed. Eventually I became willing to do what I knew was the right thing to do in spite of the opposition, the accusations and the quarrelling. I did it with the guilt of going against my husband's wishes. The evangelical dogma that man is the head of the house and "if he puts his foot in the frying pan" the woman should not say anything, contributed to my misery and guilt. Not all Christian men are so insecure that they don't value the astuteness of their wives.

Living in New York had its benefits. Since we were in an environment of mostly Caribbean people, there was an established Caribbean culture in that part of New York. On a daily basis one heard languages that were clearly Caribbean. Familiar foods were readily available. For immigrants that kind of familiarity makes relocation easier. Furthermore, our only relatives in the United States lived in New York. Very few emigrants leave that kind of cultural incubation to go afar. But we did. We were willing to leave it all behind to live in a place that we thought would enable us to live as freely as we did in Barbados. Our primary motivation was the well-being of the children.

SEVEN

Move to New Hampshire

"Tis' better to live your own life imperfectly
than to imitate someone else's perfectly."

- Elizabeth Gilbert -

A TRINIDADIAN couple who were
members of Jamaica Church told us about a
job opportunity with Christian Record Braille
Foundation, an Adventist organization. They
told us the organization was looking for field
representatives and the available territory was
in New Hampshire. They had taken the territory
that had opened in Connecticut. The leader
of Christian Record Braille Foundation in the
northeast was Elder Need. He was a dedicated
and patient man, committed to serving the
blind. He visited us in our home in New York
and after interviewing with him, we decided to

take the New Hampshire territory. Our move to New Hampshire was like missionaries going to a foreign land. We knew nothing about the place. We only knew what Elder Need told us. Looking back, it was a foolish move or a real act of faith. Elder Need made all the arrangements, including acquiring a little cottage owned by members of the Adventist church in Manchester, New Hampshire.

Again the benefit of the Adventist community was invaluable. By the time we were ready to leave New York, we were attending a new church that developed as a result of a tent effort. One of the ways the Adventist church got new members was by setting up a tent in a community and conducting nightly services. When successful, a new church sprung up in the area. Through association with this new church, we met and became acquainted with more Caribbean people. Hence our move was like a family affair. Many of the young brothers of the church volunteered their time to help us pack the truck and a few traveled with us to New Hampshire. To think that those young men and one young woman would travel the almost three hundred miles to help us get to our new destination again confirms the tremendous benefit of belonging to an organization.

When we got to our new home, our landlady had prepared a nice lunch for everyone. After our brothers and my good friend Daphne ate and were refreshed, they travelled the five hours back to New York. There is something to be said for community. Perhaps if we had stayed in New York I would still be an Adventist. However, I now understand that this kind of community is possible without the borders of certain beliefs. Embracing and serving one another just because we are 'One' would be such an amazing way to live.

New Hampshire, with its mountains, acres of farmland, ocean, lakes and rivers, was more like what I had expected America to be like. We fell in love with New Hampshire from the beginning, even learning to appreciate its long, cold, crisp winters. The sight of freshly fallen snow on pine trees was breathtaking. Although comparatively speaking the summer months were short, we valued those days when we could go to the beach, and most of all plant a garden. It was amazing how quickly vegetable grew in six weeks. The overall rugged beauty of the granite state truly contributed to it being called 'God's country'.

When we moved to Derry there was no public transportation and the closest shopping area was six miles away. Since my husband's territory covered the entire state, we had to get a car. Elder Need had lots of connections. He made arrangements for my husband to get his first car loan with a Plymouth dealer in Connecticut. The chosen car was a 1973 green Plymouth Duster. This was the easiest car we ever obtained. It was the first and only new car my husband ever owned. We kept it for nine years.

My husband loved his Christian Record job, a fact that most people cannot state. Again, it was the kind of job that allowed him to work at his own pace. The job required him to travel throughout New Hampshire soliciting funds for the support of the Adventist work for the blind. The Christian Record Braille Foundation provided talking books on records, Braille magazines and books for adults and children. The foundation also provided summer camps for the blind children. Along with soliciting funds, my husband visited blind people and recruited blind children for camp. His salary was based on how little or how much money he collected.

The job had fairly good benefits. In addition to health benefits, two thirds of the children's tuition was paid. A long-term benefit was the fact that his years of service for the Seventh Day Adventist church in Barbados were recognized. Blind camp was particularly exciting for our children because they were allowed to attend every summer. They enjoyed the swimming, boating, horseback riding, paddle boating, canoeing, and ceramics. I also looked forward to blind camp. Helping and interacting with the blind children was rewarding. Additionally, we traveled to different places in the US for conferences and retreats.

Overall, New Hampshire was a good place to live. Although we never had money, New Hampshire afforded my children childhood experiences that were unforgettable. They were extremely happy to be out of New York. Catherine's bronchitis disappeared and they had all the room they needed to play and be noisy. The little cottage we rented was down a long gravel road with woods and a brook behind the woods. Deer could often be seen. I can still see my three children now, learning to ride the second-hand bicycles they got shortly after arriving in Derry. The bikes had no training wheels and they had bumps and bruises as they determinedly learned to master those bikes.

About fifty yards across from the cottage was the home of our landlords, Mr. and Mrs. Goss. There was also a plot of land for a vegetable garden. This made my husband very happy. Our landlords had two children, a boy who was a little older than Claudette and a girl Claudette's age. The girl and Claudette became best friends and they are still friends today. They were just as happy to have playmates as my children were for them. The Gosses were white, as most of the congregation at Manchester church were. However, there was one other African American family and a mulatto Jamaican family. Things got off to a good start living next to our landlord. Not only did the children get along very well, but Mrs. Goss and I immediately developed a pleasing relationship. Since we moved there while school was still in session, Claudette and Catherine immediately began attending the Manchester Church School with their two new friends.

Our rural peaceful existence lasted four months. Late one night I was sewing (I was by now sewing everything my girls and I wore), when I heard a noise and looked out to see Mr. Goss going into the basement of the cottage. I woke my husband and told him that Mr. Goss was in the basement. My thinking was that as the man he should go and see if there was a problem. After all, we were paying rent for the place. He decided not to investigate. An electric outage quickly informed us of what Mr. Goss was doing in the basement. I was forced to stop sewing and in the morning we discovered that he had been drunk and severed the electric wires.

Yes, he was a member of the church and was faithfully attending when we moved there, but after this incident, we discovered that all was not well in the house across the way. Eventually she divorced him. We would never know if he was prejudiced, or if he was jealous of the friendship that was developing between his wife and myself. She and I had good conversations. We shared our cooking, we gardened together, and we shared the common love for sewing. We never got to see the garden mature, but she made sure we got some of the vegetables. She was a sweet soul.

Mr. Goss made it clear that we were no longer welcome in his cottage. It was too small anyhow. It had two small bedrooms, one bathroom and a large kitchen/living area. We called Elder Need and he came as soon as he could. Interestingly, at this time, the Minister of Manchester Seventh Day Adventist Church had a small congregation meeting in Hudson. They held their meetings at the Hudson Congregational Church. He had informed Elder Need that the Congregational Church had bought a house and they had an apartment for rent. Looking back on the situation, it seems that these two men knew of Mr. Goss' dissatisfaction with us living in the cottage. There was no other reason for the minister to inform Elder Need about an apartment in Hudson. They did not work together like that. Shortly after Elder Need came, Pastor Mitch came and they made the arrangements and we moved that same day.

EIGHT

Hudson, New Hampshire

"Dogmas and formulas, those mechanical
instruments for rational use
(or rather misuse) of his natural endowments,
are the ball and chain of his
Permanent immaturity"

- Emmanuel Kant -

OUR NEW home in Hudson, New Hampshire was a big three-bedroom apartment in one of the large New England colonial houses. We were now living on a busy street, as the name Central Street implies. Moving to that apartment was one of the many opportunities, I thought, we were given to enable us to better our economic situation. We lived in that apartment for six years and the rent was always $25 per week. To me this was the perfect opportunity. I continuously encouraged my husband to go to school. I envisioned education as the vehicle to greater earning power and consequently the way to make our lives less problematic.

Shortly after we moved to that house, I discovered I was pregnant. That was the last thing in the world I wanted. I was taking every precaution to prevent that from happening. I had long realized that the role of a full-time housewife, like the one I had when I was in Barbados, was not possible if I wanted to have the kind of life I knew was possible in America. I did not have high expectations, for I was never a follower of the Joneses. I remember as if it were today. I was standing at the kitchen sink when I resolved to embark on doing all I could to create the life I came to America to experience. Therefore, I cried for days when I found out I was pregnant. I was unhappy for months.

You would think that because the rent was only $25 per week that financially we would have been in a better position. Instead, things got worse. To put food on the table we resorted to food stamps. Instead of looking for another job or finding a part time job, my husband wrote to his relatives in England begging for help. How does a strong, proud, independent-minded woman maintain respect for a man who, instead of doing all he can to provide for his family, resorts to depending on others? The mere thought of begging for help sickened me. Going shopping with food stamps was most embarrassing for me. I did not come to America to be on the welfare line. My feelings towards him were not good and this was the beginning of losing respect for him as a man. If I understood the law of allowing as I do now, would I have responded differently? Maybe, but then again because of these experiences I was in constant pursuit of the meaning to life.

We were then attending the little Adventist congregation that met in the Congregational Church. The church was only three doors away from the apartment, so we walked to church every Saturday morning. Our affiliation with the church proved very helpful once more. Two members of the church owned a nursing home in Milford, a town about thirty minutes away. Although at that time I was not qualified, I got a job as a nurse's aide. In the beginning, the home was more like an assisted living home and often I worked the overnight shift by myself. I did not drive, therefore, my husband drove me to and from work. Eventually one of the owners paid for me to take driver's education, thus enabling me to get my license. I obtained my driver's license in December 1973. Receiving it liberated me to a degree. Having my license freed me from being so dependent on my husband. Boy, did that give me a good feeling. I no longer had to ask him to take me to the market when he came home in the evening, consequently eliminating one of the causes of conflict. Often when I would ask him to take me, even to get milk, he would fret and quarrel and sometimes refuse to go.

It was not as if I was sitting at home watching TV all day. In fact, I did not watch TV at all. Instead I was always busy making the most of what I was given. I continued to make clothes for the girls, Erwin and myself. I cooked everything we ate from scratch. The only can I opened was corn to make corn fritters or corn chowder. We grew fresh vegetables in the summer and what we did not grow was often available from others. In the winter, we ate a lot of carrots and cabbage because they were inexpensive and available. I made all the bread, cookies and granola we ate. The six years we lived in Hudson we were lacto-vegetarians. Therefore I was even more diligent in making sure that we had balanced meals. From Mrs. Goss I learned about berry picking and getting apples from the orchards. In blueberry, raspberry and blackberry season we went berry picking. We also went to the strawberry farms to pick strawberries. I made applesauce with some of the apples and with the berries I made fruit soup. Since the children were only allowed to consume a limited amount of sugar, they either had pure maple syrup or peanut butter with applesauce or fruit soup on their pancakes and waffles.

There were two factors that contributed to our healthy eating habits. As was mentioned earlier, in the writings of Ellen G. White, the Adventist prophet, much admonition was given on what to eat. Not as much emphasis was placed on it in New York as in New Hampshire. I came to the point where a lot of what I did or did not do had to be in accordance with what Sister White said. In fact, to ignore her counsel on eating meant you were bound straight for hell. I can remember being very burdened by the fact that my children would not adhere to the health message, thereby jeopardizing their soul's salvation.

The other factor was limited funds. Therefore we went to the orchard to get seconds, or drops. We picked strawberries because you got more for your money at the farm. We capitalized on the many berries growing in the wild. We never went to ice cream parlors because it was cheaper to buy a gallon of ice cream and a box of cones. When traveling, we rarely ate out. We took food with us and when we ran out, we went to the supermarket to buy fruit, nuts, yogurt and other wholesome foods.

We were very brainwashed during this period in our lives, particularly me. I, in my true form, was completely committed. I had given my mind completely over to this organization. We were living as the great philosopher Immanuel Kant said, dependent upon guardians to determine what we do. In my case the guardian was the prophet of the Adventist Church. Almost all my conversations with my limited friends were about what Sister White had to say about one subject or another. We were convinced that if we did not send the children to church school we would be punished. Consequently, even when things were at their worst, when the Braille organization paid a greater percentage and we still could not afford our part, the children had to go church school. By now we had three children in school. Our inability to pay meant that the church footed the remainder of our children's school fees. Not all members of the church reacted favorably toward helping people with "more children than they could afford". I was not offended by the comment, since at that time I also believed that children are the sole responsibility of the parents who bring them into the world.

Nevertheless, we became very active in the Hudson congregation that moved to the next town and became Nashua Church Seventh Day Adventists. In fact, our entire social life was church-centered. Ironically, the only black family in the church when we moved there was a couple and their two children who were also from Barbados. This was wonderful, particularly for the children. At least they had companions that looked like them. We needed the Greens more than they needed us; hence, we went to their house a lot. She was an awesome cook. It was from her I learned how to make good bread. My girls became particularly close with their daughter.

The strict adherence to keeping the Sabbath were an integral aspect of our social life. The Sabbath was truly a day of rest. On Friday we cleaned and cooked in preparation for the Sabbath. The Sabbath meal was always special, and more often than not we invited others home to share our meals and have lively conversations. Often we extended invitations in advance, but many times we took home strangers who were visiting the church that day. Then there were the pot-luck dinners. The social committee at Nashua Church celebrated and recognized everything with a pot-luck dinner. This was when everyone brought a dish and after church we would eat and intermingle. The food was usually plentiful and there were no end to the desserts. Then there was the yearly camp meeting in South Lancaster Massachusetts, the location of the Adventist Northeastern Conference. This yearly event was held for nine days. It was where you saw people you didn't see for years. It was also where you were sermonized and confirmed in your elitist position as an Adventist. In time the Greens moved there, as it was a community of many Adventists. It was also where there was an Adventist high school and college.

While transitioning to work for the Braille Foundation in South Lancaster, my husband's coworker and his family lived with us for five months. Hudson was forty five minutes' drive to South Lancaster. Although space was limited for we only had three bedrooms, we existed well together. I was working, so Donna helped with the cooking and housework. I missed her when they finally moved to their new home. After the Wines moved to South Lancaster, we often spent a long camp meeting weekend there. The children loved it. They got to spend time with their friends, the Greens' children and also the Wines' boy and girl. The children particularly liked our visit to the Book and Bible House. We usually stocked up on food items that could only be found there. Furthermore, for the book readers it meant getting a book or two. Like Erasmus, books were high on my list of things to buy.

Amazingly our low economic status was never really evident because of our association with the Adventist Church. Our children went to private school, two up to eighth grade. Only two years of Claudette's sixteen years of education were spent in non-Adventist schools. Catherine completed elementary school. As Erwin grew in understanding, he began to have conflict, even as a child, with the ways of Adventism, particularly those that were projected by the principal of the elementary school. Agonizingly, when he was in sixth grade, we took him out of Kellogg Elementary School and sent him to public school. By the time Everett was ready for school, we knew his personality was too strong for the church school. Furthermore by then we were beginning to question the doctrines of the church, me in particular.

Besides going to private school, the children had the rich and rewarding experience, as mentioned before, of going to camp every summer. We also traveled as far West as Nebraska by car. On our way we passed the great lakes of Michigan. We stopped in Cincinnati, Ohio, passed through the city of Chicago, Illinois and being used to mountainous New Hampshire, we marveled at the miles and miles of the prairie lands of Iowa.

Our time in New Hampshire was highlighted with many blessings. I now know that I did not have a true spirit of gratitude when we were experiencing them. One such blessing was the baby shower held for me shortly before Everett was born. The church members recognized my need for baby things, seeing that I was starting all over. Indeed, I felt like a first time mother, in that Erwin was almost seven years older than Everett. The shower was held at the home of one of the owners of the nursing home where I worked. They gave everything I needed, even the crib. Another such blessing was the Christmas tree and all the decorations left outside our door the first Christmas we were on Central Street, and we never found out who did it. You can imagine what this meant to the children. In my opinion, a big blessing was the fact that the children were healthy. After moving to New Hampshire, I never even had to deal with an ear infection.

Everett was born in May of 1974. Recognizing how important my attitude was to his development, I eventually managed to accept the pregnancy. I gave birth in Nashua Memorial Hospital. As with the three other children, it was a natural birth. The doctor and nurses were amazed that I refused everything they offered. My reasoning was, in Barbados nothing was available and my previous births were fine. Why do anything differently? What was cruel though, was the act of tying my hands to the bed, hindering me from rubbing my belly. I suppose they thought I would lash out when the pain became severe.

He was a beautiful, big baby, with lots of hair on his head. He had so much hair that even though he was a boy the nurses tied blue ribbon in it. There was nothing newborn looking about him. He weighed 8 pounds, 14 ounces and measured 22 inches. There was not a wrinkle on his skin. It was smooth and perfect. His presence drew nurses from different floors who wanted to see him. Why were they so interested in seeing him? I could only imagine it was because he was not only beautiful, but he was black. He was not only beautiful, but he was strong.

The day after he was born, as he lay on his stomach in the little box, I saw him holding up his head and looking around. I dared not mention it to anyone, for from my experience, babies' heads were not so strong. It was only after the head nurse mentioned it that I knew I was not seeing things. One nurse loved him so much she visited us after we went home. While most newborn babies lose weight, he never did. He grew very fast and was always tall for his age. Today he is 6 feet, 6 inches tall. When we were in the supermarket, people would always stop and admire him. One day a lady came up to us and after commenting on his good looks, she touched him and said "soft." Were the tables turned, I wonder what the reaction would have been.

Months after Everett's birth I went back to work. It was imperative. After I went back to work my husband suggested that we do what was necessary to continue getting the food stamps, but I was anxious to put them behind me. I opted to work the third shift because I was making money and at the same time I was able to run my household. It was not too difficult when Everett was a little baby, but when he started to move around, it was tough. In the morning I would get in the bed with him and try to read to him. I would dose off and he would poke my eyes out. When he started walking it was worse. I remember many mornings wondering if he was ever going to grow up. It never entered our minds to get a babysitter; the expense would have undermined the purpose I was working.

We were surrounded by lovely neighbors, but I was always too busy to idle away any time with neighbors. Eventually I became pretty close with one. Sue and I developed a relationship after Everett was born while I was not working. Our common interest was sewing. She looked to me for advice on her projects, because I was the more experienced seamstress. Eventually, when Everett was in his terrible twos, she would sometimes watch him for me so I could get some sleep. Another neighbor who Everett hung out with as he got older was Raymond Smith. Raymond and his wife Virginia lived directly behind our garden area. He was a kind Christian gentleman who was retired and enjoyed having the boys around. When school was out Erwin hung out with him also. Virginia was very concerned when Everett was a baby that he was not getting enough nutrients, since we were vegetarians.

When the other children were home it was

easier, for they all took care of Everett. Summer was wonderful, for I would come home in the morning and write a list of chores for each of them, then I would go to bed until noon. When I got up the house was usually sparkling. My older three learned early how to do things in the house. My rationale was, if I had to work, then everyone had to pitch in. The tradeoff was—particularly in the summer—when I got up we often did something special, like going to a park, or go berry picking. As they got older and went into the working world, they were always commended for their ability to perform their work well.

For me the years spent at 25 Central Street were full. The children grew and their needs increased, and so did my frustration. I was particularly frustrated at not being able to provide for the children the advantages necessary to succeed in this world. Claudette, I found out after the music teacher came to our house and pleaded with us to allow him to give her private violin lessons, was musically talented. He went as low as $5 a lesson. I was not working at the time and my husband said he couldn't afford it. I wanted him to afford it.

There are some opportunities you don't pass up and to me that was one. It was years later when Claudette's youngest son demonstrated the same musical propensity that I understood why the music teacher came so far to beg us to give him that chance.

With the help of Mrs. Goss' daughter she taught herself how to play the piano. Therefore, I became determined to get her a piano. The opportunity came when I made a jacket for one of the members of the Congregational Church and he paid me $75. With that money in hand, I looked in the local paper every week, until I found a piano teacher who was selling an old upright for exactly that amount. The piano was in excellent condition. Years later when we were leaving New Hampshire, I sold it for $95. In the meantime, for a while my cousin in New York paid for Claudette to go to piano lessons.

The children learned at a very early age not to ask their father for anything. He would always fuss and sometimes go so far as to tell them that he didn't have a father to call upon when he was small. I found it so difficult to understand how a man with seemingly all his faculties, no encumbrances, could be unaware of his role as a father and husband. I would never forget when on our way to Lincoln Nebraska we stopped in Ohio and met a gentleman who was dumb, blind, and deaf. He had a PhD, and was the head of an organization. His only means of communication was to make signs in the palms of his assistant's hand. I was so inspired by this man and his accomplishments. I remember thinking *My god, if this man could accomplish so much, what the hell is wrong with my husband that he is so complacent and satisfied with so little*?

His dealings with Claudette were definitely differential. Many times I was caught in the middle. It was so bad that the year Everett was born and she was eleven, I asked my uncle in Canada to adopt her. My uncle wanted a baby, therefore he declined. As she developed into a young lady, the piano became her salvation. She spent endless hours taking out her frustration and anger on it. At the age of sixteen her unhappy existence manifested in her developing an over-active thyroid (I am of the firm opinion that all diseases that afflict us result from dis-ease of one kind or another). Consequently I could not wait for her to finish elementary school. For me there was never any doubt that she was going to attend one of the Adventist boarding academies. Not that I did not want her at home, for she was a very capable and helpful child, but I was reaching for peace for all of us.

Ironically, my spiritual understanding at that time, which was supposed to bring me peace, brought none. I was totally dedicated to 'serving the Lord' as the Christian church put it. I hungered and desired to live on a higher plain, as one of the songs said. I diligently read, I prayed, I studied, and yet peace evaded me. I would go to hear preachers speak and just cry my heart out. Compounding my situation was the fact that I was still so guilty about my childhood experiences. One of the things that was a source of discomfort for me was the fact that my children were so big and I was so young. For this reason, I was ashamed for anyone to know my age. Additionally, at this time I also felt that I was the one totally responsible for the lack of marital happiness. I would question myself as to why I couldn't be different. Why did I have to be the way I was?

My inner turmoil, along with a lack of sleep, was not good. Often distracted by the heaviness of my situation, I ran through many red lights. One night on my way to work I went to sleep behind the wheel and awoke to the car tires crunching the ice on the other side of the street, and the car facing in the other direction. As I became cognizant of what had happened, an eighteen wheeler came whizzing by. On all these occasions, I concluded that it was not yet time for me to die.

Naturally I was getting older, and likewise gaining more understanding about life. In the meantime my feelings toward my husband became more negative. It got to the point that I was happy when he was working far away and did not come home every night. I tried really hard to present a good front, but those were days of deep inner conflict. As a result of the inner turmoil, I looked for whatever inspiration I could find in books. From one of these books I learned that the difficulties in life could be beneficial. It took many years before I understood that my failure to accept was what created my misery.

This was also the time I began to seriously question the Seventh Day Adventist doctrine. In particular, their interpretation of Daniel 8:14, the Investigative Judgment and the Kingdom of God. The church's interpretation of this scripture along with the fourth commandment was very significant to the church's claim of peculiarity. Shortly after I began to question the doctrine, I heard about an Adventist minister from Australia who was preaching a different interpretation of this scripture and consequently he was asked to give up his credentials. I ordered his tapes and found that his interpretation answered every doubt I had. This was the beginning of my lack of faith in Adventism and to a certain extent my lack of faith in organized religion.

I have the type of personality that it is either all, or nothing. I would be the one to throw out the baby with the bath water. I had zealously embraced Adventism as the only truth. To find out that such a key aspect of their doctrine was flawed and could be interpreted differently provided the license I needed to move beyond the borders of thinking the church imposes, borders one gladly accepts when the belief is: 'I have the truth', or 'I belong to the only true church'. Amazingly, most of these Christian organizations do not teach you to listen to your true self. In fact, they separate you from the real you. To follow your feelings was not the right thing to do. Years later I would learn from the Barbadian mystic Neville Goddard, that *Feelings is the Secret*. I was at the time unaware that the path to enlightenment meant letting go of old beliefs as light is shed upon them.

The housing committee of the congregational church did not have in mind that families would live in the church's house indefinitely. They bought the house with the intention of enabling families, by charging low rent, to afford their own house. After we were there for six years, they made it known that it was time for us to go. However, they were willing to do all they could to help. By now my strong intention was to move into my own house. While working in Concord, the Capital of New Hampshire, my husband learned that a new housing development was being built. With the help of the church we acquired the necessary downpayment and signed up for one of the houses. This did not materialize because the builder went bankrupt. Thankfully, one of the members of the Church's housing committee was a lawyer and he was able to get our money back. In the meantime, another member's mother's house became available in Pembroke, a small town outside Concord. We were offered this property to rent with an option to buy within a three year period.

We moved to Pembroke in 1980. Everett was six years old and quite a handful. My most vivid recollection of our first days on Pembroke Hill Road has to do with him making decisions, even at that age. We had been lacto-vegetarians all his life, so he had never tasted meat. The first week we were in Pembroke, he became friendly with a little girl in the neighborhood. One evening at supper time he could not be found. When I did find him, he was on his way home with a satisfied look on his face as he licked his lips. When I scolded him for not being home for dinner, he said to me, calling his little friend by name: "they were having chicken for dinner and I wanted to taste it." I can still remember the look on his face as he said it. All I could do was laugh. Truthfully, for me the days in Pembroke were particularly consumed with Everett.

Our house on Pembroke Hill Road was the oldest house in the immediate community. It was a quaint New England, two-storey cottage with a detached garage. I never learned the exact history of it, but it was old enough to have horse hair walls and slate siding. The structure was sound, but it needed updating. There were four unheated bedrooms upstairs. Downstairs had one small bathroom, a living room, a large kitchen/dining room area and another room we called the multi-purpose room. Many of these New England cottages appeared to be houses that additions were made to from time to time. This one was no different.

The house was situated way back on a half-acre lot. Consequently we had a lot of front lawn to cut. Our backyard did not go too far, but adjoining it were three acres of woods owned by our landlord. The boys spent many enjoyable times in those woods. To the right side was enough space for our summer garden. To the left was a row of fir trees that separated us from our neighbors and provided privacy. There was a continuous stream that ran in front of the fir trees. Eventually I planted a beautiful wildflower garden in the immediate front, next to the porch. At the end of the long driveway was a large oak tree where Everett and I sat and ate lunch on many summer days. The long driveway meant lots of snow to shovel. The house was truly a handyman's special.

I became the handyman. The first thing I encouraged my husband to do was to pay someone to refinish the little bathroom. I had readily found a job at McKerley's Nursing Home in Concord and almost immediately made friends with the maintenance man, named Barry. His first job was refinishing the bathroom. After that, because money was always a factor, I devised a plan to get Barry to do the work that was beyond my ability and I did the finishing. Hence, I learned to spackle dry wall, and paint and hang wallpaper. The most difficult project was the replacing of the horse hair stairway walls. However, I learned how to make scaffolding that enabled me to reach the high places. I wallpapered all the upstairs bedrooms except the master bedroom. I wallpapered the living room, slip covered the furniture and made beautiful curtains. After a rain storm caused the roof in the boys' bedroom to leak, I convinced my husband to spend the insurance money on fixing the ceiling in their room.

I was on a solo mission to transform that

house. Solo because I was met with much opposition from my husband. Everything was possible for me and everything was impossible for him. I did not let his opposition stop me from accomplishing my mission. Getting the things done without his approval did add feelings of guilt for not being an obedient wife.

When I went to work for Northern Telecom I saved $25 every paycheck. When it accumulated to $200, I paid Barry to do one project after the next. I stripped and painted the entire front porch with help from other members of the family. I replaced the lattice around the porch. When my husband got hit from behind in a car accident, I pleaded to use some of his compensation to add new siding, arguing that it would raise the resale value. I used this same argument to spearhead getting a member of the Manchester Church who was an electrician to put electric heat in all the upstairs bedrooms. Luckily, Ed donated his labor and the materials.

Claudette came home when we moved to Pembroke. So she and Catherine attended Pembroke Academy together. She only had two more years in high school, but being minorities they were good company for each other. During this time they also worked with me at McKerley's Nursing Home. At first they both worked as kitchen aides. After Claudette went off to college Catherine became a certified nurse's aide. This concerned me because I knew how hard nurse's aide work was, but she was in her element, since she had always aspired to be a nurse.

When Claudette graduated and went off to college, Catherine surely missed her, and the fact that she was an outsider became more apparent. She was not part of the crowd that had moved through the school system together. Eventually, she did become friends with two students who were also newcomers to the Pembroke Academy community. I appreciated those girls very much. They were two level-headed teenagers. I needed that because the boys were difficult. Everett alone was more trouble to raise than the three older children.

Erwin was bright and very capable, but as he progressed into his teenage years he became more and more rebellious. He made the honor roll his first semester in high school, but after that he just read books. By this time I was working full time hours and Everett was demanding much of my attention. I received calls from his elementary school almost every day. I recognized Erwin's needs at this time, but my plate was full, so I supported him in every way I could. When he was playing basketball, I went to all his home games. I recognized that at that developmental period in his life, he needed a mentor. His father would have been good, or someone like a big brother would have helped. Erwin never got the mentoring he needed.

It was at this period in my life when I realized that although I had a husband, we were on different pages when it came to raising the children. I was of the opinion that husbands and wives worked in chorus to provide the economic, social and emotional needs of their children. But that was not my experience. I lived for my children, while my husband's attention was focused on his needs. I bought books and we talked about what was needed, but he never caught on. He admitted years later, after we were divorced, that I tried to make him understand, but at that time he didn't understand the need for him to be an active father.

Everett was a squeaky wheel and he got the grease, from me at least. He was a head taller than most of the children his age. He was a big, black, strong-willed kid in a lily white school. Therefore he stuck out. Even in kindergarten he recognized the difference and would ask, "Why couldn't I be white?" This prompted me to think that he would benefit from being in Barbados, where people with his color were the majority. I was very burdened with his behavior and Erwin's non-compliance.

After Ma gave me the go-ahead, in 1982 I took him to Barbados. I was relieved not having to worry about him. Ma was glad to have him, but it only lasted a year. He was too much for Ma. There was no male help there either. I find it hilarious that many men claim a position of authority, but when it comes to dealing with the difficult issues they shy away. Perhaps they don't have the capacity or the know-how to deal with difficult situations. Such was my experience, and as a result I would tell you I raised my children by myself. Anyone can go to work and bring home a few dollars, but it is the giants that get in the trenches and help combat the enemies that raise their heads sometimes when rearing children. Many Christian men spend endless hours in the mission field while their wives are single-handedly contending with the most important mission field, the one at home. An absentee father is not necessarily one that is not living at home. He can also be one who lives at home, but has very little interest in the day-to-day workings of the home. When he is not working, he spends his time sleeping, or going to meetings and sitting on this and that board.

While Everett was in Barbados, I started going to college. I had received my GED while we were living in Hudson, with the intention of someday attending college. I did well in school, but did not quite grasp the concepts of digital electronics. I would have done better in a traditional semester school. An eight-week turnaround was too fast for me at the time. I did receive my Associate degree in 1985, which enabled me to get a better position at Northern Telecom. I however lacked the basic skills needed to become a technician. Nevertheless, acquiring the degree increased my earning power and I was able to move away from house cleaning and working 11 pm to 7 am as a nurse's aide.

Claudette graduated from high school in

1983, and she and her siblings went home to Barbados. She and Catherine bought their tickets, I paid Erwin's way. When they returned, they brought Everett back. My relief was over. The difficulty of the years that ensued I still cannot find the words to express. He became even more insecure, because in his eight-year old mind, I had sent him home because I did not want him. However, as he aged he was grateful for the experience. Since he does not want to be considered anything but a Barbadian, the year he spent there gave him perspective. He now appreciates has firsthand knowledge of Barbados.

In Barbados he did well in school. Consequently, when he returned he was well ahead of the children who were in his kindergarten class. However, when he returned to school in America the next school year, he was placed in the lowest second grade class, even though we had his workbooks showing his level of progress. He would come home and complain that it was as if he was in kindergarten all over again. "They have me counting with beads," he would say. He came back from Barbados with a mastery of his 'times tables'. His workbooks showed the level of multiplication and division he had mastered. The arrogance of America caused the school to place him in the lowest second grade class. After all, he had spent a year in Barbados, a third world country. The attitude of the principal was, there was no way he could have learnt as much as the children that stayed in America. He was not seen as an individual. From that experience I realized how the American educational system keeps children back, how the ability of young children are undervalued. I fought with the school for weeks to get him placed in third grade where he belonged. The best I got was a higher second grade class. In the meantime, the daily telephone calls resumed. Only the universe knows whether if he had been placed in a class where he was challenged and not bored, if he would have behaved better.

His behavior caused them to put him through all kinds of tests, but I refused to let my child be pigeon-holed. Although at that time I was not willing to deal with it, I now know that some of his behavior was due to our dysfunctional home. He was a brilliant child who was very big for his age. At eight years old he was the size of a man, hence more was expected of him. He also reasoned like an adult, a trait in children that is difficult for most adults to deal with. If children were understood to be little people and not extensions of anyone, we would be more respectful of their individuality and relate with them accordingly.

Recognizing that I was very much like that as a child, I had compassion for him. I understood that as he got older he would find his place and I continued to believe in him regardless of how badly he behaved. I never condoned his behavior, but I gave him reasons to believe in himself. Understanding that he was misplaced in New Hampshire would eventually be the driving force behind our departure from New England.

When living in Pembroke we moved our membership to the Concord Seventh Day Adventist Church. We were still strongly adhering to the rules. The children were older now and things were not as orchestrated as when they were small. There were so many schedules to juggle that finding time for formal family worship was difficult. I don't think the children were sorry anyhow. I was still very busy going to school, working full-time, cooking everything from scratch, and still sewing for the girls and myself. My husband had taken over the bread making. During the two years Claudette was home, she and Catherine were very helpful, even though their lives were full.

While we lived in Pembroke, the summers were exciting. Many friends and family visited us. We established a pattern of going to the White Mountains every summer. We never got tired of driving up the Kancamagus Highway, watching the Sabbath day falls; seeing the Basin and the Man in the Mountain. Any place of interest that my husband learned of in his travels we would visit. We visited Lake Winnipesaukee, the playground of the well-to-do. We climbed Mount Washington. We went to the Cathedral of the Pines, the Mica mines and the Rhododendron State Park, where there are acres of beautiful rhododendron flowers. Living in New Hampshire truly enriched the lives of the children. In the winter they enjoyed the snow. We never went skiing, but they enjoyed sledding and ice skating.

For a brief period in our lives I did not have to carefully check the prices of everything I bought in the supermarket. This was when I was working at Northern Telecom and my husband was working two jobs. Both of his extra jobs I found in the newspaper. I was the lifeline of our home, even though that was not what I preferred. I would have given anything to follow. But there was nothing to follow. For me to follow, you have to be leading me somewhere. It finally dawned on me in 1985 what was the major contributing factor to the conflict in the marriage. For in spite of all the seemingly beautiful things we did, there was constant conflict and I was miserable. In 1985 we went home to Barbados together for the first time. His sister was home from England after sixteen years. After that visit, I gained clarity. I then realized the major contributing factor to the conflict. It was as if I was on top of a hill constantly trying to pull him up to where I was; truly an impossibility.

Is it possible for two people to live happily ever after with two such diverse perspectives on life? True, all couples have their differences, but there has to be some synchronization at some point. The only thing my husband and I had in common was Adventism. The borders of my world were large and ever-expanding; with him there was no vision. My lack of tender feelings towards him was evident. While the member of the Nashua Church who told me about Desmond Ford was going through her divorce, she came to live with us. She and her youngest stayed with us for five months. After her façade had fallen apart we had developed a relationship. She said to me one day after being there for a little while: "you don't love your husband, do you?" She was right, but I don't even remember what I said to her. It was not easy for me to admit that to anyone. I wanted to love him. He was my husband. I tried, but I would always end up at the same place with the same feelings. Hence, I ask the question, when two people fall in love, is it just choice?

Catherine and Erwin came of age in Concord. Catherine adhered to all the rules and Erwin broke all the known and unknown ones. After she was accepted at Georgetown University in their nursing program, she received one of the largest scholarships anyone at Pembroke Academy ever received. If she had listened to the guidance counselor at the school, she would not have applied. I suppose he did not think that a poor black girl could get into Georgetown. He did not know their mother. My children grew up knowing they were going to college. The conversation was not about 'if', but 'when' you go to college. When she told me what he said, my advice to her was, "if that is where you want to go, than you should apply." After she was accepted and the guidance counsellor heard how large her scholarship was, he was proud to spread the news. The husband of Christa McAuliffe, the teacher in space, graduated from Georgetown. Since Georgetown set their freshmen up with an alumni, he was the one recommended for Catherine to meet with.

With Catherine off to college it was just Erwin and Everett. My girls were peaches compared to these two. They presented some serious challenges. Erwin was a very rebellious teen and Everett was a strong-willed, big child. Experiencing them taught me that each child is unique and that each child comes into this world with their own set of needs. Most often adults fail to meet these needs because we believe that when it comes to raising children, what is good for Peter is good for Paul. Dealing with Erwin's issues taught me how to deal differently with

Everett. One important thing they taught me was that public school was not helpful. I often wish I could have homeschooled or sent them to Montessori schools. They were both very smart and forward-thinking children. Hence, the school system that treated every child with the same expectation was hard for them. This was particularly true of Erwin. He eventually was kicked out of school six weeks before graduation. All he needed to graduate was English. Therefore I took him to Manchester every morning, enabling him to finally complete the requirements for his Pembroke Academy high school diploma.

Since Everett was a generation younger than his siblings, he spent many of his childhood years alone and he was bothered by this. It bothered me also, but I was glad to be working days. To make it worse, he did not have any friends in the Pembroke community where we lived. There were a few children from the school in his age group, but they never became friends. Was it because he was black, or was it because we were the poorest in the community? Eventually, Kyle moved into the neighborhood across the street, and the two became fast friends. Their favorite game was dungeons and dragons, much to my dismay.

It is interesting to note that he and Catherine had similar issues when it came to making friends. In both situations their problem was solved when another new person moved into the neighborhood. For the two years Claudette spent at the high school she made one good friend. Erwin was the social butterfly. Perhaps it helped that he played basketball. In my opinion, New Hampshire was a close-knit society. If the children started kindergarten together and continued their schooling together it was very hard to break into those cliques.

Our situation was compounded because we were black, as Everett's experience proved. Everett's social issues were the impetus behind our decision to leave New Hampshire. His lack of friends and the many hours he spent alone gave me visions of him growing into an overweight, very unhappy teenager. The only solution I saw was to move to a more cosmopolitan community. By then Erwin was in his senior year of high school, about to join the Marines, and thus the decision to move was sealed.

NINE

Move to Dover, Delaware

Why do you move to all those strange places?

AFTER SPENDING one year in New York, we left all our cultural support and moved to the cold and pristine beauty of New Hampshire. Then after 13 years we pulled up stakes and moved, this time to a place just as remote as far as Caribbean people were concerned. Remember, Brooklyn and New York were the familiar locations for most Caribbean people. Our choice of Dover, Delaware prompted my brother, who was then living in Canada, to inquire, "Why do you move to all those strange places?"

When we left New Hampshire in July of 1976 the weather was still wet and gloomy, so we particularly welcomed the warmer weather of Dover. The first December in Dover we raked leaves instead of shoveling snow. The Dover location was convenient to those we needed to visit. Claudette was farthest away in Massachusetts and she only had one more year in college. We were now closer to Washington DC where Catherine was, and not too far from New York, where my relatives lived.

After visiting Dover, Delaware and recognizing that it was a multi-ethnic city, our decision was made. We put the house on the market and it sold in a very short time. My ideas and hard work had paid off. We'd bought it for thirty nine thousand and sold it for more than twice as much. While waiting for the closing, we visited Dover to go house shopping. We made contact with a real estate agent, hence we had choices when we got there. We quickly settled for a four bedroom colonial. It was a lot more house than what we had in New Hampshire, and we only paid sixty-eight thousand for it. It was a very nice house on a fairly big lot. The backyard was big enough for a vegetable garden, which was very important. Even then the house needed some updating, but the only remodeling we did was to add some cabinets between the kitchen and family room, thus creating a sitting area where we used bar stools.

Eventually, after helping to pack things up, I moved to Dover first in order to prepare the house for our move. My husband, the boys and the cats came later. Claudette was on her own at college in Massachusetts. To pay what remained of her tuition after Christian Record paid their part, she took out student loans and worked very hard to maintain herself. Catherine was also on her own. She joined the Army ROTC after her second year at Georgetown and received a full scholarship. Besides the heavy load of studies as a nursing student she now had added responsibility of ROTC.

Erwin joined the Marines and a few months after we moved he was off. Living in the big four bedroom house were my husband, Everett, myself and the cats, Pansy and Midnight. One would think that economically life would have been easier, but it became serious. My husband's secure job was not so secure. The relationship he had established with the business community in New Hampshire was not being repeated in Delaware. Hence, for months his salary was $95 a week. Eventually, he was forced to find another job and just like years before in Barbados, he took a job selling insurance.

I know a lot of men and women who made a substantial living selling insurance. My husband was not one of them. Therefore we continued to struggle economically. I was constantly asked to wait until one thing or the other happened that would increase the cash flow. Of course, none of these things ever materialized. In the meantime, Everett became my sole responsibility. He knew that asking his father for anything would often generate an argument, so he came always to me. My performance as dutiful wife was beginning to wear thin. After more than twenty years of working hard to maintain the facade, I grew weary of it. One of the things I stopped doing was ironing his clothes. I was one of those women who made sure my husband was fed, his clothes were taken care of, and all his needs were met. I was not a career-minded woman. In my mind my primary responsibility was taking care of my family, but I came to believe I was the enabler. As I struggled to keep on top of things, he slept. He was at peace with his inability to provide for us. As time went by, the house needed a roof, the bathroom had a serious leakage, the front door needed replacing, and the kitchen cabinets were falling apart. I eventually bought a front screen door and got my stepfather, who was visiting, to put it on. After all those years I was still hoping that my husband would exercise the leadership that is expected of men.

As for me, after moving to Dover I could not find a job. I worked for a little while at a department store reconciling invoices. When that did not work out, I went back to working as a nurse's aide. I decided to go back to school to become a Licensed Practical Nurse. I was funding it with some of the money that remained after we bought the house. That came to an end when my husband, without discussion, took all the remaining money out of the joint account and put it in his name, so I had no way of paying for the courses I needed. I was still paying student loans for the Associate Degree I received in New Hampshire and did not want to accrue any more debt. Working as a nurse's aide ended when my husband won tickets to Disney World and my job refused to give me the time off. I took the time, and when I returned I found another job working in a tailor shop.

Except for the brief moment I went to needlework when I was an adolescent, I had no formal training. Yet, from the time I began to use patterns to make my clothes, it was noticeable that my finished product was exceptionally well done—no homemade look, thus causing me to conclude that I was gifted in this area. Consequently, I developed a faithful clientele. Eventually, the tailor shop was not making enough money to pay me and satisfy the expectations of the original owner. When he started talking about closing it, I had already started proceedings to take over. Therefore I began to make the necessary arrangements to become an entrepreneur. I registered the business in the county and in the state. I ordered a new sign, and in April of 1989, much to the surprise of the original owners, Dover Tailor Shop became Elaine's Tailor Shop. I owned and operated my shop for seven years. Sometimes I had as many as three people working for me on a sub-contract basis.

Managing my own business was a very

important part of my evolution. It was labor-intensive, the chance of becoming rich was slim, but it afforded me autonomy. In 1990 I moved it from its original location to a more desirable part of town. Contributing to this move was a remarkable, elderly white female customer. She encouraged me to move to South Bradford Street, into the house across the street from her. She felt the location was better for business. Ms. Mark was a very independent, shrewd woman who had left her husband and branched out on her own when it was not the fashionable thing to do. She had also once owned her own business. Eventually she gave me the sign she opened her business with. It was made in 1948, the same year I was born. I still have the sign. After I moved across from her, she looked out for me. When she noticed me dragging out of the shop late in the evening, she called me and told me about a very expensive, but good vitamin to take. The strength she exuded at her age inspired and encouraged me.

The new space I rented was a cozy, three-room apartment with a front entrance in a very large multi-dwelling house. I worked long hours in an effort to make the tailor shop successful. I particularly liked the customer service aspect of the job. I developed an excellent rapport with my customers. As a result, I never had to advertise. Meanwhile I also developed a good relationship with the white Anglo Saxon protestant male who lived directly behind me. He was very prejudiced, and he told me so. He was a captain on a tug boat and was gone a lot. Sometimes months would go by before he came home. He was also an alcoholic, but he would become valuable to me as time went by.

My husband's apathy fueled my feelings of hopelessness and despair. My unhappiness and dissatisfaction increased. I felt truly trapped. I cursed the day I was born. The Christian hope in a future heaven was all that kept me going. I bought two pictures with two African American girls looking up with tears in their eyes, one said, "God will wipe away all tears from my eyes." I hung them in the foyer of our house where I could be constantly reminded of my hope for the future. My husband hated them, but they truly expressed the sorrow that was in my heart. I was at a place familiar to many women of my era. Fear of God, children, economics and our concern about what others think so often kept us bound to these very unhappy situations.

One day in 1987 I was traveling on the highway, driving Claudette's car, when I was rear-ended. She had recently graduated from college and was vacationing in Barbados. I suffered no noticeable physical defects, but shortly after I became severely depressed. It was as if I were in a deep hole. All the joy went out of my life. There was no smile on my face. My eyes were dead. I found crowds or crowded environments impossible to negotiate. I remember going to the Adventist camp meeting that summer and all I wanted to do was lean against a pole. I had problems sleeping at night. I wanted nothing to do with my husband; so I moved out of the bedroom. Lorraine, my childhood friend who lived in New York, came to visit. We went to Washington DC to visit the Capitol Building and I had to lie on a blanket under a tree while everyone else visited the building. I was incapable of climbing the steps or facing the crowds. I then was convinced that I was ill, but I believed my sickness to be physical. Therefore, as soon as I could I went to a general practitioner.

We had not yet established a family doctor, since we were basically a healthy family and there was no urgency in doing so. Consequently, I went to one of those family clinics who at that time charge a flat fee of $96. The young attending physician I saw immediately recognized my problem, and that same day sent me to the mental health clinic. I supposed he noted the urgency of my case. Without an appointment I was able to see a psychiatrist. She diagnosed me as being clinically depressed and prescribed 25 milligrams of an antidepressant, which took effect immediately.

I was also assigned a counselor. Not far into our counseling sessions, as I expressed to him my frustration with my partner, he asked if I ever considered getting a divorce. My response was: "I will never get a divorce." In my Christian mindset divorce was not an option. Although my marital experience had been a miserable one I was determined to continue the façade. Ironically, in looking back, I realize how much my illness would contribute to my decision to get a divorce.

I turned forty in 1988 and found myself pregnant. Another mouth to feed was not even an option. Neither of us wanted another child. It was agreed that I would have an abortion and get my tubes tied. I never gave having the baby a second thought. I had struggled so hard with the other children, all the time hoping for my husband to step up to the plate, and I knew it was too late for change. Furthermore, my husband had confronted me with this question: "what are you doing for your financial future?" That was a question I never expected to hear from him. I suppose I was still of the opinion that he was the financial provider. In the meantime, we were forced to get the equity out of the house to pay off our consumer debt. The equity was substantial, for we had made a twenty thousand dollar downpayment. Included in that debt were two student loans, mine and his. He had attended New Hampshire College and received a degree in one of the Human Service fields. He however never did anything with it. Working in the human service field necessitated working 9 to 5, and he was never interested in working set hours. In spite of the evidence, I somehow continued to believe that my faithfulness as a wife and mother guaranteed that my needs would have been met. I believed that for far too many years.

In the meantime, the move to Dover was good for Everett. His fifth grade homeroom teacher, his first homeroom in Delaware, was a male teacher who recognized he was a live wire and kept him in check. He however had an English teacher who put him out of her class almost every day. In spite of his issues in her class, he thrived. In sixth grade he was the main character in his English class production of Othello. He wore my dress and carried my pocket book, as he also acted the part of Othello's aunt. Besides being an excellent student, he played basketball all his junior and high school years. He was the big man and was heavily depended upon in all games. He also played in the band. I missed none of his performances and very few of his basketball games.

Unlike his experience in New Hampshire where he only had one friend, he made friends in Dover. His first best buddy was the son of the principal of Dover High School, who was white. Then Everett became black conscious and developed a cadre of black friends, and he still keeps in touch with many of them. Altogether, his school days in Dover were much less problematic than in New Hampshire. I was his rudder that kept him on course. I begged and borrowed money to send him to basketball camp. I allowed him to use my car to go to Philadelphia and to Wilmington Delaware to play in the basketball leagues. Eventually he was noticed in his junior year of high school, and he was courted by a number of colleges. In the end he accepted the full basketball scholarship offered by LaSalle University.

In 1989 Catherine got married. I made her dress and all the bridesmaids' dresses. Many of my relatives came to Dover for the wedding: all those who lived in New York, my mom and my cousin and his children from Barbados, and all my family from Canada. It took Claudette a little longer. Eventually, she married in 1995, also in Dover. Catherine's daughter was then old enough to be the flower girl and her son was the ring bearer. Again, I sewed all the dresses and my grandson's jacket. Many of the relatives attended just as they did for Catherine's wedding. As a result of his training in food service in the Marines, Erwin did the catering. My uncle in Canada was the officiating minister. Our family doesn't have family reunions, so our weddings and funerals always feel like a family reunion.

Although I worked long hours in the tailor shop, I continued to maintain my domestic duties. I particularly made sure that Everett's needs were met. For his junior and senior prom, I made his clothes and his date's dresses. I eventually came to the place where I felt that my family were the five children and myself: the four I gave birth to and one I married. The four I gave birth to grew up and took on more and more responsibilities. Meanwhile, the fifth one, my husband, I was going to be stuck with for the rest of my life. By now it was clear to me that I no longer wanted or was willing to 'wear the pants'. Erwin returned home around this time and recognized that I was only going through the motions of being married. By the fall of 1992, when Everett was ready for college, I had changed my mind about divorce and was ready to make a move. I was mentally divorced a long time before I finally made the move to get a divorce.

Having clarity about what I wanted was one thing, but doing it was a totally different matter. I agonized over my decision for months. Fear was at work. I feared what others would say, particularly my very religious family. I had no reason to be afraid of how I was going to be economically provided for because I had been taking care of myself for years. I went for counseling, not because I was hoping to mend my marriage, but because I needed help in working through my resolve to end my marriage. I was looking for validation of my decision. The emotional pain was real. I wanted out, but according to the Christian dogma, I had no grounds. There was no adultery involved, hence, according to the church, I had to stay. No wonder the breakup of my marriage and my separation from the church were simultaneous.

In spite of the fact that the divorce rate is so high, there are still many women and men in relationships that sap their very life force. Most often money and religion are the determining factors. Much physical and emotional sickness and dis-ease could be averted if people were only taught that they are the creators of their world, their every experience. If I had only known that the God within is the only true god, the God from whom we must take our guidance.

Although I did not have the conscious understanding of the power that is innate within all man, I felt that there was something within me beckoning to emerge. After all, my childhood was problematic. I had moved from childhood into adulthood never getting the chance to know myself or how to make choices and decisions just for myself. I always deferred to one person or the other. It seems as if my spirit was saying: "It is time to get to know yourself." It was time to take the road less traveled.

TEN

Divorce

You have to live in a house without closets before
you know how much you like closets.

- Abraham Hicks -

I LIVED for my children. I found total pleasure in raising them. They kept me going during the twenty-eight years of my marriage. It is then no surprise that the desire to break up my marriage gained momentum after my youngest had gone off to college. In 1993 I was in my forties with no economic security. I had the strong belief, however, that I could take care of myself. It never entered my mind that I was too old to be on my own. Perhaps it was because throughout the twenty-eight years I was married, I had learned how to stretch a dollar. Therefore I figured I could continue to do so on my own.

Owning my own business gave me the impetus I needed. When the apartment two doors down from the shop became available, I attempted to rent it. I did so tentatively, because getting a place where I could live and work presented an opportunity for me to leave home, but I was scared. The owner however, wanted more rent than I was prepared to pay, so I had to leave it alone.

I started to sleep in the tailor shop more often. In the meantime, I had befriended the white guy who rented the apartment adjoining the tailor shop. With him being gone for months, I seized the opportunity and asked if I could use his place. The tradeoff was, I had to keep the place clean. It was a good arrangement. When he was gone I used his apartment anytime of the day, but when he was home, I went into the apartment quietly, very early in the morning and took my shower. When he was not drinking Sean was a likable guy, but he was unpredictable when he was drinking. One never knew what was going to come out of his mouth. That was the only problem I had when he was home.

In time I introduced him to my Barbadian

cooking and we sometimes ate dinner together. In the end he was glad for my company, because he really did not have any friends. After the owner of the place I originally made the offer on offered it to me for the right price, I moved the tailor shop. In typical Sean fashion I heard: "I really miss your ass." Admitting he missed interacting with me was big. After observing me working so hard to make the tailor shop a success, he confessed that I gave him a different perspective on black people. Before knowing me, his view of black people was that they were lazy and no good, as his father had taught him. Maybe in a sense you can say I was infatuated with him, but that was as far as it went: a thought.

Elaine's Tailor shop at 119 Division Street was nicely set up. I sectioned off one side of the large front part of the apartment as my work area, and the other side served a double purpose as my living room and my waiting area for the business. A new sofa, nice window dressings, decorative mirror and a few pieces of artwork added to the décor. The middle section had only one large room and a passageway that led to the back room which became the kitchen and dining area. I hired a carpenter to build a closet in the large middle room and it became the bedroom.

Informing the children that I was separating from their father was met with varying responses. They understood why I was doing it, but with the exception of Claudette, it was difficult for them to think that we were not going to be a family anymore. Claudette felt it should have happened much sooner. Erwin had seen it coming for a long time and wondered what took me so long. Everett, the youngest, said: "mom if you have cancer you cut it out." Catherine, on the other hand, took it very hard. She, for one reason or the other, never saw it coming. Claudette and Erwin were very much aware of my misery, hence they were not surprised.

My decision did not affect my relationship with Claudette and the boys, but it set a great gulf between Catherine and myself. Ironically, she and I had the closest relationship, and it was severely breached after the divorce. For twenty years until I remarried she continued to believe and to pray that her father and I would get back together. She told me she had no problem with me separating, but the divorce was a sin. My very religious relatives took the news with more candor than I expected. My aunt, who had become my mentor, said "I hate even the word divorce," but she understood why I would grow tired of trying to make a bad situation work. My mother said: "It is your life, you are the one who is experiencing it. You have to know what is best for you." I did not need their approval, but the mostly positive response emboldened me.

According to Catherine, I was bitter when I left, but in truth and in fact, I was not really bitter. I was angry at my husband for all the wasted years, but what she interpreted as bitter was my stern way of making it known that I was serious. Knowing my ex-husband, I knew that he would make my life miserable if I had continued to communicate with him on friendly terms. Therefore I communicated only when necessary. If and when I did, it was not very cordial. Indeed the divorce was hard for him, and at first every opportunity he got he would tell me the reasons why I could not leave. The first thing he did was to give me a Bible with all the verses highlighted that condemned my actions. He called me one day and told me that

I was forty-five, I would be forty-six in a year, pretty soon I would be old and I was making a mistake branching out on my own. Without telling or warning me, he dropped me from his health insurance policy. I believed he thought that would be enough to force me to return. Nothing was going to change my mind. I had too long dreamed of the freedom I was enjoying. Since leaving, it has not always been easy, but I have never regretted my decision, neither have I missed anything from my marriage.

Catherine became her father's prop and he leaned heavily upon her. He was so affected by the separation that his health began to deteriorate. It took him years to come to grips with his new status, but he eventually did. He now says that I did him a favor, because I forced him to grow up. He confessed to making my life miserable. He admitted to not being a real man. He also recognized that he was only half the father he could have been to the children. Although he says he understands that our relationship is over, I believed only my remarriage would end his hope.

Not too long ago he offered me the economic security of his pension. What I find difficult to understand is why he would want me back when he knows that I do not love him. Over the years he knew how miserable I was. I told him on more than one occasion that if I had grown up before I got married, he would not have been my choice. Our relationship is cordial and relaxed when we meet. He calls me and I talk to him. However, I have no intention of ever formulating a relationship with him, no more than his being my children's father and we are connected that way.

As a beautiful butterfly emerges out of a cocoon after a period of incubation, my incubation period was about to begin. I had read somewhere that the human body begins to break down after thirty-five if it is not exercised. Therefore I embarked on an exercise routine. Every day between 12 noon and 1:00 pm I closed the shop and went to a lunch time aerobics class, held in the armory. I changed my eating habits. I added more fruits and vegetables to my diet. When the lunch time program ended, I joined the gym. The exercise that was most effective for me however, was walking. I would sometimes lend my car to my son, which meant I had to walk to the gym.

One day I decided to stop spending my money and just walk for exercise. As a result, my mid-section became noticeably smaller. Women young and old began to comment on how good I was looking. One of my friend's daughters said to me one day: "Ms. Elaine, you are born over." I did feel as if I was born anew. There was a freedom in my spirit that I had never realized. I began to pay more attention to my style of clothes. I always had a sense of what was flattering to my body's style, but I became even more aware. The real Elaine was emerging and it felt good.

I was separated for a year before I started dating. The person I started seeing I had known for years and had never noticed how handsome he was. During the years I was married, I never paid that kind of attention to another male. I was totally faithful. He was pleasant and talkative and so was I. Hence, when he brought clothes to be tailored, we chit chatted. The new me got his attention. This was the period when my children had opened a Caribbean restaurant in town. Often, when I went to pick my lunch up, he would be there. We would exchange pleasantries and I would return to the shop. I began to notice that he was uncharacteristically stopping at the shop. It finally dawned on me that he was interested in me. Never leaving anything to chance, I asked him. He confessed his interest and invited me to his house. Therein, as far as I am concerned, began relationship that contributed significantly to my evolution.

Jon was like a gardener who cultivated a garden that had potential, but needed his artful eye to bring out its potential. It was not a perfect relationship, but he made me feel good about myself. He particularly helped me to see my long, slender legs as assets. He helped me to feel comfortable in my own skin. We would talk about many things for hours. Eventually, he came to my shop for lunch every day during the week. Jon was a professor at the university in town. He had a broader vision of the world than I did, hence I benefited from his world view. His diction was perfect and I loved listening to him talk.

In the beginning of our relationship, he said that I was the woman he was looking for all his life. He liked the fact that besides being intelligent, I understood duty and had no problems serving my man. Most importantly, they say 'a way to a man's heart is through his stomach'—he enjoyed my cooking. He also said that I turned his world upside down. I believed him, but in the end he did not have the guts to do what in his heart he wanted to do. You see, he had a child from a woman in another country and although he never promised marriage, she expected it. He never stopped coming to see me after she and the child came for a visit. Two weeks before she returned to Africa, the child came to him and asked, "Are you ever going to marry my mother?" Thus he again accepted his responsibility as he had done in both of his failed marriages. Like Abraham Lincoln, he let circumstances do his deciding. He was good to me and losing him was painful. We share awesome memories and will be friends forever. He always said: "It was as if we had shared a life together in some earlier period."

When I filed for the divorce, it cost me $75. One of my customers who was a lawyer filled out the necessary paperwork for me. All I had to pay was the filing cost. I suppose our process was easy because I was making no claims. I was aware that I had rights to half of his pension. My feeling was and still remains that a man has a right to be able to live after divorce, unless there are children involved and he is well off. What right have I to economically burden him? I had always worked, and as mentioned before, I had strong convictions about being able to provide for myself.

All I desperately wanted was my freedom. I verbally asked that my husband sell the house after Everett graduated from college, and split the equity fifty-fifty. That never happened, because my husband did not keep up with the mortgage payments. Therefore, he gave the house back to the mortgage company before Everett graduated. Many would be surprised to hear that after being married for twenty-eight years, I did not miss my husband for one moment. Never was there a time when I said: "If he were here he would do this or that." This is because he never lived for us. He lived for himself and wherever we fitted in, he was okay with that. He was consumed with his comfort. I bore the sole burden of providing the comfort of the children and myself. Yes, he was there; yes, he always worked and he never smoked or drank; but was that enough? What about the physical and emotional support my children and I needed? The consensus of opinion is that a successful marriage requires each partner to contribute fifty percent. During my twenty-eight years of marriage, I felt the marriage was 99.9 percent me. I have since learned that in a truly successful marriage both partners give one hundred percent, one hundred percent of the time.

For years I felt as if my marriage was the biggest mistake of my life. I suppose that feeling was in accordance with my beliefs. Since my beliefs have changed, I see it as one of the experiences I created for my soul to evolve into knowing who I truly am. I learned that the principles of the universe are attraction, intending, deliberate creation and allowing. These principles work even when we are not cognizant of them. Having this knowledge, I can take responsibility for all of my experience, even my unhappy ones. I understand that I attracted a co-dependent husband because of my great need to have someone depend upon me.

Since I was so young and from a culture where at that time getting a husband was such a big thing, I intended a husband and a home to call my own and got one. I knew nothing of my creative powers, of being able to create the life that I wanted. I trusted and believed in a God outside of myself that mandated every circumstance in my life. Not knowing my creative ability, I was very reactive. My vision was very limited. Hence it took many years for me to decide to allow my husband to be himself. In seeking a divorce, indeed that is what I did. I was finally able to free myself and him from the bondage that I knew limited my creative self and possibly limited his.

ELEVEN

College

The journey of a million miles starts with the first step.
- Chinese Proverb -

HOW CLEARLY I remember the day we took Claudette to college at Atlantic Union College (AUC) in South Lancaster Massachusetts. Always a lover of learning, I remember thinking that day what a wonderful experience it must be to live on a university campus, particularly one such as AUC, with tree-lined streets and a seemingly very peaceful environment. I had a nostalgic view of college campuses. I saw them as places where young people interacted and where real education happened. Of course at that time I believed that I would only have such an experience vicariously through my children. I was content because I had lived so that they would accomplish more than me. I was rewarded with the possibilities of their accomplishments and Claudette was charting the course for the other children. If someone had told me that day that not very far in the future I would get the same opportunity, I would have doubted. In the end I would not only go to college, but I lived on a college campus and became totally immersed in college life.

The tailor shop had served its purpose. If I had never owned a business, I am almost sure I would have never gotten a divorce. It empowered me; it got me thinking of possibilities. It however was labor-intensive and the income was not enough to cover health insurance. I was beginning to think about going back to school. I believed that getting an education would have given me greater earning power. I mentioned it to Jon, since I was thinking of starting when Everett graduated from college. He thought I should not wait and he made it possible for me to take my first class in the September of 1995. In the meantime, one evening I ran into a fellow seamstress in the fabric store. She informed me of her new position as assistant resident manager on the Campus Delaware State College, which became a university later. Before speaking to her, I had never thought that there would be any job on a college campus I could do without qualifications. The conversation peaked my interest, and I became determined to apply for a housing position.

As providence would have it, shortly after that conversation the evening manager of the housing department came to my shop. I seized the opportunity to talk about the job possibilities and he encouraged me to apply. I applied and got hired. Ironically, I got hired for the same position that my acquaintance held. She was fired shortly after we had the conversation. At first, because I was hired to work the evening shift, I thought I could keep the tailor shop by closing it a little earlier. It worked well for a while, but then it became too much. Meeting the deadlines of my customers and working until 11 pm was beginning to take its toll. Therefore I closed the tailor shop in September 1996, six months after I was hired. I moved onto the college campus. By closing the tailor shop, I disappointed many of my customers who had learned to depend upon my excellent tailoring. This was the beginning of another phase of my life.

My apartment in one of the girl's dorms was great. It had two bedrooms, a lovely bathroom, a tiny kitchen, and an appropriate living room/ dining room area. I moved onto campus when it was being beautified. Consequently my living area, which had a large picture window, opened onto a beautiful man-made pond, tree-lined road and a wooded area. The window opened toward the West. Therefore I watched many sunsets through that window. The view might have been lost on many, but I truly appreciated it.

I lived in one resident hall, but I worked in the boys, girls and the co-ed hall. My main responsibility was to enforce the regulations of resident life. In this role I was often at loggerheads with some of the students. In addition to monitoring the halls, I presented programs. I gave speeches, I counseled and advised students. I worked with some international students to reestablish the International Student organization. I was truly in my element here. I was impacting lives and I was happy to be doing so.

The job was rewarding. However, I was

amazed by the apathy of so many of the students. This was not true for the many Caribbean and African Students. The American students demonstrated very little love for education. Many wanted good grades without putting in the effort. The emphasis was on getting a degree so they could get a job. What they failed to realize was that a noticeable lack of education, even though they had a piece of paper, did not make them competitive in the marketplace. The apathy towards their education bothered me tremendously.

Every opportunity I got, I reminded them that our ancestors suffered to gain the rights to learn to read and they were failing to capitalize on their opportunity. What became evident for me was the fact that because college doors are now open to students from all strata of society, there is a need for grooming students for the real world. Teaching in two different inner city settings made this even more evident for me. Many of the students from these areas have very little social references. Hence there is the need for colleges to offer more than book learning.

As mentioned earlier, I was already taking a class when I started my job on campus.

Free education was one of the benefits after your probationary period. I was impatient for the three months to end. I started working in March, so when September came I was ready to enroll in the Social Work program. My lack of belief in my inability to learn math guided me to choose a major that I believe did not call for a lot of math. I avoided math like a plague. I told myself I could not do it. Years later, when I was studying for the Praxis Math test, the test you took to enable you to teach, I realized how much of an aptitude I had for learning math.

The first two years I was working in resident life I was the only female among my co-workers who was going to school. It was interesting that many of them worked at the college for more than twenty years and were not motivated to take advantage of the free education. This was not so for me. I was like a pig in mud. I loved learning and I became the ultimate student. I went to school every semester, summer included. I was determined to make the most of my good fortune. I switched majors after completing the first year, because nothing piqued my interest like the study of the history of social work. Furthermore, the immediate summer after that I read *The Road to Coorain* by Jill Kerr Conway, an Australian female historian, and I was hooked on studying history.

You will recall that my formal education in Barbados ended at primary school. This accounted for the fact that although I had an Associate Degree, I still struggled with the written language. My poor command of the English language was compensated by my tenacity and resolve. I persevered, and class after class, I got better. Many of my grammatical errors were due to the fact that I did not understand many of the basic principles of the English language. It was my Barbadian vernacular that significantly impacted the way I wrote. I am thankful that my professors were diplomatic enough not to discourage me. I suppose my strong determination and zeal to learn gave them confidence in me.

As a result of my experience, I know that anyone who wants to badly enough, can succeed at college. I did not find college hard, I found it challenging. But I reveled in the challenges. Writing was something I did naturally. It came naturally for me to tell someone how I felt in a letter, even as a child. I can still remember the first letter I wrote to a boy named Eric. I know that I can express myself better through the written word. I even wrote letters to my children and husband when I had a problem with one thing or the other. Ironically, although I lack the deeper knowledge of English principles, I can read someone else's writing and tell them what is wrong and suggest a better way to express it.

One of the last research papers I wrote to fulfill the requirements for my Bachelor's degree was an independent study paper on how and why Barbados became independent. I was able to persuade one of the leading English professors on campus to edit it for me. He assured me that I could write. He was not the type of person to speak idle words. Therefore I believed him and was encouraged. He was an expert on the English language and his critique was encouraging. He commended me for the construction and the fluidity of thought. His words were: "I have colleagues that cannot put their thoughts together like this." He did say that it lacked commentary, which he said would come as I acquired more knowledge. How right he was!

I have come to see providence in my switching

from social work to history. If I had continued studying social work, I would never have honed my writing skills. Being a historian forced me to write better and better. Self-confidence also played a significant role in my writing ability. I found that after I believed in my ability to write, and I didn't need the approval of others, my writing has improved significantly. I still make some of the same mistakes, but a lot fewer.

The small salary I made on campus was sufficient because my living expenses were few. I was still helping Everett. In fact, when he needed a car I was the one who bought it and made the monthly payments. I however insisted that he help when he worked during the summer. I supplemented my income by sewing for some of my old customers and because I kept my business phone number, I acquired new ones. Some of the female students benefited from my presence, for I hemmed, altered and even made entire outfits for special occasions.

I was otherwise involved with other activities on campus. My big project was the international student organization. I was actively involved with its success from 1997-

1999. I volunteered my time and worked with the students in planning and implementing all of the programming the organization carried out during that period. My apartment was often abuzz with the Caribbean students. What primarily drew the students to my apartment was the food. The aroma of the Caribbean food caused knocks on my door, with the question: "Ms. Catlin what are you cooking?" In addition to the students I shared my food with my co-workers and campus security. From time to time, some members of the housekeeping staff would bring the ingredients for me to make them a pot of curried chicken, everyone's favorite. In addition to this, I threw birthday parties for students. If I knew someone had the flu, I would make them a pot of chicken soup. I truly enjoyed serving all who I could while on campus.

Living on campus had its disadvantages. In addition to not having privacy, sometimes in the wee hours of the morning someone would maliciously pull a fire alarm. This meant that I had to throw on a bathrobe and go outside until security said it was safe to return. That was particularly problematic when I had an early morning class. I usually slept in because I did not have to be at work until 3 pm. One day I caught a student climbing through my window. After that, I kept it half-open. Except for that incident, I felt safe living on campus.

All in all, life on campus was good. During the time I was working on campus I travelled to somewhere different every Christmas holiday. The last place I went to was to Norway. It was the year after Everett graduated from college and he was playing ball there. Letting no opportunity pass me by, I took advantage of this one and got to see a part of the world that I would otherwise have no desire to see.

I bought my first computer in 1998. Words cannot describe the relief and the assistance it brought me. I did not depend on it for my grammar, but it has been a meaningful tool in helping me to overcome some of my difficulty with the English language. I know I would not have gotten this far without it. Since I could not type, I depended on others to do my typing for me. I came to realize that I was asking too much of others. My thoughts were: *Why should other people care about how well my work is done*? They normally didn't. Since I take pains to do for others as I would do for myself, I was rudely awakened when I depended upon other people to help me with my typing. Eventually I bought a Mavis Beacon tutorial typing CD and practiced typing.

At first I was intimidated by the computer. Claudette was my first tutor. As time went by, I went to workshops to learn how to use some of the Microsoft functions. I remember that the instruction seemed like Dutch. However, as little by little my confidence and comfort level rose, I eventually taught myself how to use many new functions. I know without any doubt that I would not have been able to attend graduate school and complete a Master's program without the invention of the personal computer. It made writing the many papers I had to produce easier. Of course I had to make many corrections, but the computer guided me and made the task manageable. My children marveled as I gained computer proficiency.

My time at Delaware State University was also a time of personal evolution. For so many years I hated my type 'A' personality. From childhood I was conditioned to feel that I had so many faults. It was while living and attending school at Delaware State University that I began to see and appreciate my personality for what it is. It was then that I began to realize that in truth and in fact I had much to be appreciative of. In addition to my ability to learn readily, I can put the most delicious meal on the table in a short space of time. I can efficiently clean on a white glove level. When I tailor something, the finished product is superior. I am well read and I can communicate on many subjects in addition to being an able speaker. In other words, everything I do, I attempt to do it well. One can only imagine how frustrated I was when my writing skills were unsatisfactory. Given my personality and my determination, I only needed time to get better. It is not my intention to brag, but I have learnt to affirm myself, because for so long I was criticized and condemned for being me.

When I was at Delaware State University, I began to appreciate my body. All my life, I hated my body. Most of my adult life I did not like what looked back at me when I looked in the mirror. It was not because I was so ugly, it was because I hated myself. I believed the voices that told me I was wicked and evil. I believed the voices that made fun of my long, slender legs. I believed the voices that made negative remarks about my breasts that pointed more to my feet than straight ahead. I believed the voices that made negative comments about young women who became sexually active at an early age. Many of the voices were the voices of relatives and people close to me.

At this time I pursued physical fitness as eagerly as I pursued education. Every day, sometimes twice a day, I would walk around the track. At least three times a week I walked up and down the bleachers and in the winter I walked the stairs in the tallest residence hall. Consequently my legs, though not much bigger, gained greater definition. As a result I began to feel comfortable in shorts and shorter skirts. When I did wear shorts, men and women alike complimented me. I discovered at this time that longer shorts did not compliment my long legs. I gained enough confidence to wear them at a shorter length. Jon's daughter saw me in my white shorts one day and said: "Man, Elaine you don't even have any cellulite." At fifty, my legs had found their place. I finally was not ashamed of them.

Education can be a powerful tool for good. Epictetus said hundreds of years ago: "Only the educated are free." I am not only talking about a formal education, but about the acquiring of knowledge. As I became more and more aware, many of the fetters that kept me bound and hateful of myself fell away. The most important step I had to take was freeing myself from the conceptual prison I was locked away in for the greater part of my life. Unquestionably, my divorce and my move away from mainstream Christianity happened simultaneously. Did I move away from the beliefs of my childhood in order to make room for a divorce which was condemned by those beliefs? Perhaps! However, I have no regrets. For in throwing off those beliefs I have gained an understanding of the 'God' that I would never have found if I had remained blinded by those beliefs.

I did well in my studies, graduating with a 3.65 grade point average. I became a member of the University's Honor Society and the History National Honor Society. The Saturday morning I sat among all those young people on the football field at Delaware State University waiting to receive my Bachelor's degree, I was fifty-one years old. The speaker for the occasion was Johnny Cochrane. I don't remember a word he said, but at the time I thought what he said was important—good admonition for the graduating class.

At my age, who would give up a secure job and go off to graduate school? I would, and I did! The journey has been tough, but my development as a result of the knowledge I have gained and the people and circumstances I have encountered are invaluable. Still I did not make the decision without trepidation. Of particular concern was health insurance. I was at the menopausal stage of my life and leaving Delaware State would mean giving up good insurance coverage. I learned that most colleges had clinics, particularly colleges such as Howard that are affiliated with hospitals. Therefore, with the encouragement and help of my professors, I applied and was accepted at Howard University.

In my mother's wildest dreams she would have never imagined that she would live to see the day when she would attend my college graduation, but she did. She was not only there, but she prepared all the food for my graduation celebration. Happily, it was well attended. My children and my grandchildren, my brother and his family, came down from Canada. Many of my professor friends came, and my aunt came from Florida. I would err in not mentioning my friends from the outside community, including my ex-husband.

TWELVE

Graduate School

To repeat what others have said, requires education; to challenge it requires brains.

- Mary Pettibone Poole -

MY TREPIDATION about going to graduate school turned into excitement and anticipation when I was accepted into the history program at Howard University in Washington, DC. I applied to a number of schools, and Howard was the last place I applied to. I did so at the bidding of one of Howard's star students who came to teach in the history department at Delaware State University. He recognized my potential. I believe I owe it to him that I was admitted into Howard University. I was not only accepted, but I also received a letter informing me that there was no record of my application for scholarship. So I did apply and was granted tuition remission and a monthly stipend.

In August 1999 I moved to Washington DC. By sheer coincidence, Everett was offered a teaching position in Washington DC. So the two of us rented a truck and coordinated our move. When one of my mentees at Delaware State University heard I was moving to DC, she told me that her stepfather was remodeling a multi-dwelling house, and would have apartments for rent. Fortunately, the apartments were ready by the time Everett and I had to be in DC. Our new homes were adjoining garden apartments in Anacostia, in the South East section of DC. The crime rate at that time in Anacostia was very high. So negative was the perception of where I was living that when my relatives came to visit they were surprised at how nice my apartment was and how quiet the location was.

On a graduate school stipend, I could not afford much. Therefore finding a one-bedroom apartment with living and dining areas, kitchen, bathroom and nice hardwood floors for $450 per month was perfect for me. Anacostia is one of the most picturesque sections of DC. It was unfortunate that drugs and crime had given it such a bad reputation. However, when I moved there in 1999, the area was getting better and the crime rate was going down.

We looked out our front window into a wooded lot that was seemingly beautiful in the summer when the leaves were on the trees. In the winter when all the leaves were gone, it became an undesirable sight. It was a dumping ground for the lawless. While we were there, our street was not without incident. One morning a dead body was found in a bullet-ridden parked SUV one house away from us. Another morning we woke up to find Everett's car demolished by a hit and run driver. I believe that the accident was purposefully orchestrated by a student who was kicked out of Delaware State University under my watch. She was caught in a dorm room with five male students smoking pot.

The benefits of moving to the South East part of DC far outweighed what most would consider the negatives. Moving there next to my student's parents gave me instant friends and a kind of moral support. This was quite a different experience from moving into an apartment and not knowing the people whose doors open a few feet away from yours, and you never see them or get to know them. My son was on one side and my Caribbean friends across the yard. This made me truly comfortable living in the South East. We never had to worry about where to park our cars, or which side of the street to park them on. Public transportation was convenient. Furthermore, Anacostia and Howard were on the same metro green line. Getting a few parking tickets motivated me to use public transportation. In the end it was also cost-effective and practical.

Our apartments were in an eight-unit garden type apartment building. Our landlord owned four of the units and someone else owned the others. Everett and I were on the first floor. Two brothers lived above me, and a young man I will call John, lived above Everett. There was one general entrance to the four apartments. Therefore the door was usually left unlocked. The first Sunday morning I was in DC I went for my walk, thus continuing my walking routine. This particular morning, I did not take my keys with me. I had left my apartment door unlocked, knowing that the front door would be unlocked. Not this particular morning, John, the guy upstairs, had gone for a ride and when he returned he locked the front door. Finding myself locked out, I called up to him, because I knew he was the only one that was up. When he came to let me in, he happened to mention that he was getting ready for church. I said, "Yeah, what church do you go to?" He said, "Unity." I became very excited and asked to go along.

I became excited on hearing Unity because after leaving the Adventist Church, I visited many churches. There was no Unity Church in Dover, Delaware or in close proximity. Therefore, I had never visited one. I was visiting the churches with the hope of finding a congregation where I was comfortable. I knew of Unity through the Daily Word, the little devotional booklet the organization publishes, but I knew little about the doctrine.

I cannot remember what the minister talked about that morning, but from that first Sunday I knew that I would be going there often. I had no interest in joining any organization. As a result of my total brainwashing by the Adventist church, I pledged never to give my mind over to any man-made belief. I however heard different ideas at Unity. I heard the last part of a chant the minister sang on entering the pulpit. It ended with these words, "... and your God is my god and our god is one." Here I recognized openness, an embracing of everyone's beliefs. I further heard, for the first time, someone praying to mother/father god, thus taking away the patriarchal god, presenting a god who represents both the masculine and feminine.

These words also captured my attention: "There is only one power and one presence in the universe, god the good, individualized in you and I as the Christ." Many would shout 'Blasphemy!', but it made more sense to me than the ideas taught to me from childhood. It substantiated an all-powerful god and not a god who competes for power with a force he created. In my opinion, it was likewise empowering the individual. It gave meaning to the words of Jesus, "Greater things than these you will do, because I go to my father". Those words, if really repeated by Jesus, demonstrates that he recognized that each and everyone has his same capacity to experience the power of the universe.

I think the most attractive of all the practices at Unity was the positive affirmation of the person. This was so contrary to my experience of always hearing how sinful I was. Rather, at Unity the Christ-self was affirmed. Most notably in the words of the song, "I behold the Christ in you, I see him as you walk, I hear him as you talk…" This is only one of the many positive affirmations heard each Sunday at Unity in the nation's capital. Much hope and assurance is found in the verse that closes every Unity service if you ever attend.

It is as follows:

> *The love of God enfolds you.*
> *The power of God protects you.*
> *The presence of God surrounds you.*
> *Wherever you are, God is and all is well.*

My failure to attend church was a concern for my mother. She, however, was even more concerned when she heard I was attending a Unity Church. Like the majority of us, she feared what she really knew nothing about. All she knew was what someone had told her. Never having set foot in a Unity Church, she knew nothing of the blessings that are so abundant there. Amazingly, we humans think that our all-powerful God needs us to protect him, and the truths we have constructed to be his truths. Hence she meant well when she believed I was keeping company with 'the devil'.

I received an excellent education at Howard, but I value just as highly the spiritual guidance and understanding I gained at Unity. The two years spent at Howard gained greater significance because of my introduction to the Unity organization. The things I heard there contributed greatly to my understanding of life. In my opinion, the founders of Unity were onto something when they started Unity. They grasped a bigger picture of 'God', but as with all organizations, the members failed to recognize that they can keep adding to the light that was given to the Filmores. This was not true of the founder of Unity in the nation's capital. He propounded the light he had been given. I often wonder how he remained a Unity minister; his message was so different from many of the other Unity churches I have attended. It was never bible-based or Jesus-centered.

Shortly after my introduction to Unity, I met an amazing gentleman on the internet whose father was from Barbados. Donald's primary interest in trying to connect with women on the internet was to share the empowering truths he had come to understand. Therefore, he gave me the book by Donald Neal Walsh, *Conversations with God: An Uncommon Dialogue.* This book shed light on the spiritual truths I was already beginning to understand.

At first, so much of what my friend was saying made no sense to me. It was from him I learned to take responsibility for everything that I believed happened to me. He introduced me to the laws of attraction and creation. I had difficulty at first understanding how an innocent child could intend or create the horrors of my childhood. It was only when I understood and believed that I am not just this form, but indeed, I am a bigger self—a self that is connected to all that is, to what man calls God. This truth helped me to accept responsibility for all my experiences. As a result, I try not to blame. By not blaming it is easier to embrace and to forgive others. Even when I blame, because it is so easy to fall into old patterns, eventually I come to terms with my role and my creation of what is.

Naturally, learning not to blame meant that

I also had to learn not to judge so harshly. I remember Donald clearly saying, if you see things as neither bad nor good and as just an experience, life becomes easier and you will become less judgmental. Reading Conversations With God helped me not to be ashamed of the fact that I found sex rather enjoyable. In fact, when it came to my sexuality, I was totally dwarfed. My new understanding was like a door opening; the wider you open it the more you see. In this case I wanted the door opened, and the more knowledge I gained the wider the door became.

At Howard my grammar was not perfect, but I saw the deeper truths in much of the history I learned. For some unknown reason I could see a metaphysical perspective where others did not see one. This was also true at Delaware State University. I remember that when I gained a more in-depth understanding of Atlantic slavery, I was able to compare the pain of it to a mother giving birth. Who dwells on the pain after the life is celebrated? Now I know that as God beings we create all experiences for greater purposes. I did not then have the spiritual clarity I now have, but something within me spoke to a deeper truth. When my professor was bewailing Booker T. Washington, I saw Washington as an aware person who at the time understood what was best for his people. At Howard I understood Atlantic slavery not as an anomaly, but as just another aspect in the evolution of the world we live in. In the meantime, as I learned the history of pre-colonial Africa, I saw a correlation between Africa's colonization and the colonization of the Americas in 'God's' name. I also realized that the Jews' claim of God giving them the Palestine land also has a familiar ring.

As I said, the door was opened. As I learned more about the early history of the world and the evolutionary process of culture, the clearer it became for me that what I thought was the truth was really not truth. It's never easy to let go of old beliefs, but when you are being compelled to do so by the many coincidences and synchronizations, you have to change. As a result of the study of early history, I also came to the realization that all civilizations have their myths. Just as our belief in a triune god seemed real, theirs was equally as real to them. Even though we now think of the Greek gods as unbelievable characters, someday, in another civilization our god myth will also be laughable.

I will never forget the morning I was cleaning and watching public TV. Joseph Campbell was being interviewed by Bill Moyer. I had never heard of Joseph Campbell, but I knew that one of my more recent thoughts was, our civilization needs a new myth. As I listened, those exact words came out of Campbell's mouth. You know, that ended my cleaning. What these two were saying resonated with my thoughts, therefore I listened.

I volunteered at the Martin Luther King Library in Washington DC while attending Howard. Being single, I was looking for a way to socialize with others of like minds. While thumbing through a magazine I found at the library, I came across an advertisement for a monthly meeting of spiritual singles in Silver Spring. The lady who chaired the meeting had attended one of Eckhart Tolle's first talks in the US in 1999. She was so impressed by him and what he had to say that she opened her small home to all who wanted to attend. The place was usually crowded.

Since it was around dinner time, many of us ordered food from a Vietnamese restaurant. While we ate, we listened to the audio tape. Afterwards we would discuss what we heard. Again, I was being confirmed in my new understanding. Furthermore, as one who was a clinical depression sufferer, I needed Eckhart Tolle's truth of living in the present moment. I particularly needed to be aware of my thought system and how it derailed me. From him I learned that my clinical depression stemmed from me being addicted to my thoughts. His explanation of the 'pain body' was real for me. According to the medical profession, once clinically depressed, always clinically depressed. I argue against that, for when we learn to bring our thoughts into subjection, we also bring our depression under control. We are first and foremost spiritual beings and second physical beings. I am convinced that being controlled by thoughts results in most mental illnesses.

I graduated in 2001 and I am truly grateful for my graduate school experience. If it were not for Dr. Harewood, there is a strong possibility it would have taken me longer to find my way. I actually was in a PhD program, but as my spiritual understanding evolved, I felt no need to obtain this title. Furthermore, my blood pressure went through the roof while I was at Howard, so I quit with a Masters. The Caribbean professor who was my advisor was a political and economic historian. I definitely was not interested in political and economic history. I learned my interest when I read Howard Zinn for a historiography class. My thoughts resonated with his social history perspective.

It was providential that I became Dr. Harewood's teacher's aide. It was the experience I gained from proctoring her classes that enabled me to formulate the aspect of Caribbean history that motivated me. Eventually, classes she created aided me in finding my way. Funny thing is, she was not liked by most graduate students, but I liked her. She was no nonsense, yes, but she was systematic, methodical and on top of her game and I respected that.

The dichotomy within me was very evident while I was at Howard. In some ways I demonstrated self-confidence, for without confidence I would not have entered graduate school at 51years of age, particularly since

I was lacking the traditional background. On the other hand, I was very negative and lacked belief in myself. It did not help that my Caribbean advisor made it evident that he thought I was out of place. I am grateful for the Howard and Washington DC experience. Being there exposed me to the information which has aided me in my continuous evolution as an aware being. And as Aristotle said: "Educating the mind without educating the heart, is no education at all."

THIRTEEN

Growing in Grace

*"You have come to this World in this way,
at this time, in this place,
to know who you are—and to create
who you wish to be."*

- Neal Donald Walsch -

I GRADUATED from Howard in 2001 with great expectations. I envisioned getting a teaching job that would pay me more than I had ever earned. I foresaw having more money to give, living comfortably, traveling and doing the things I enjoyed doing. It did not happen quite like that. I know that I had the intelligence to teach, but I never considered the behavior of the children. Nothing could have prepared me for the modern classroom, particularly an inner city classroom.

My first teaching job was at a charter school for at-risk children, in Washington DC. I taught twelfth grade world history. I was surprised to find that many students could only read at the third grade level. I gave this my best effort, which was not good enough. It was not the adjustment of teaching methods that I found problematic. It was the rights of bad behaved children, whom you had to honor in spite of their unacceptable behavior. It was then that I became aware that schools were more about the façade of learning than real learning. In other words, school was about putting up a front to enable it to qualify for government money. I also learned that to be a successful teacher you had to have a strong sense of self, which I lacked.

After the first year I quit and returned to Delaware, believing that teaching would be easier there. What I did not know was that Bush's "no child left behind" was going to make it hard for me to get hired. Schools were now required to hire only certified teachers. Even though I had a degree in history, it was not enough.

I was then depending on friends for a place

to live, and willing to do any job I could find. I found a job working at a call center. What an eye opener that was! I found favor with the floor manager who was black, but the top manager had difficulty with my proud bearing. She treated the call center helpers with disrespect. It did not take her long to realize that I was not going to be disrespected. She did everything she could to get me fired. She more than once called my line pretending to be a truly obnoxious customer. The floor supervisor understood it was her and advised me on how to handle the call. When she was unable to trip me up, she found a trumped up reason to get me fired.

That center was at that time mostly selling for a popular young women's store. Immediately following my dismissal, I wrote the company a letter informing them of the unlawful way the center was being run. My complaints were substantiated. Consequently, shortly after she fired me, she too was fired. I was not prepared for the kind of slave environment that existed in the call center. Often, the persons who manned the phones in call centers were high school dropouts or people who felt they did not have a chance in life. Hence, they tolerated unfair practices.

I eventually worked as a substitute teacher in four Delaware school districts. In time, I got a long term eighth grade American history position. I loved teaching, I believed that the teacher learned just as much, if not more, than the students. However, how do you engage children who were more interested in the opposite sex than what was being taught in the classroom? This was my first middle school experience. Clearly these students were more interested in the opposite sex than in learning. From this experience I became convinced that children during this time of puberty could benefit from single sex schools.

At this school children were given fifty points when they entered a new grade so their chances of failing were lessened. In my class there was a sixteen year old, an excellent motor mechanic, who had no interest in book learning. He believed the fifty points were unethical. But meeting those qualifications set by the 'No Child Left Behind' mandate set the precedent, forcing schools to do whatever it took not to fall behind.

My only child to complete all public school grades was Everett. I was totally committed and involved in his education. However, I did not have a clue about the zoo-like environment I was sending him into when he attended public school. It is no wonder so many children drop out. I actually called him one morning and apologized for subjecting him to the public school environment. I think if many parents understood what the public school environment is like, they would engage more in their children's education. They would not commit their children solely to people they really don't know.

This was in 2003. I worked that summer on Delaware State University campus, teaching writing to Upward Bound students. In the meantime I kept hoping to find a secure job. In August of that year I moved to Charlotte, North Carolina where my eldest lived. I continued to diligently look for a job. I eventually found a job working at a historically black College as a dormitory manager. This school has since lost its accreditation. I was amazed it was accredited when I was there. There was definitely no real education going on there. It had one history teacher for five hundred plus students. The top girl in the school asked me to edit her resume. It was so poorly written that it gave evidence of the poor quality of education she was receiving.

Since all my working experience was in the North, I was not prepared for the Right to Work law in the South. I gladly worked the Thanksgiving holiday and was expecting to get Christmas off. I bought my ticket as usual, and was ready to go to Barbados to visit my mother. However, in the south you didn't get the same kind of rights I was used to in the North. I had worked for three years in residence life at Delaware State University and never did I have to work a Christmas Holiday. Therefore I was expecting a similar kind of treatment at this school.

Since I treated the students with respect, many of the girls who lived in the dorm with the head dormitory manager wanted to move to my dorm the next semester. The rules and regulations of this school were still in the dark ages. Residence managers were expected to micro-manage the students—to manage the students in a way that not even their parents could be successful doing. There were many antiquated expectations that were put in place when the school was run by a religious organization. For example, students were forced to attend a 6 am Christmas morning service. As dormitory manager it was my duty to see that they attended. The other dorm manager bribed her girls to go. I did not realize that I had to bribe grown women to do what they already knew was expected of them. Although I made two rounds to wake everyone up on time, very few of my girls went. I guess I did not fit in at this southern school. I was an excellent dorm manager, I just didn't belong there. Working there was a step backwards, literally, on my life's path.

Once more I found myself jobless and feeling hopeless. I was desperately looking for work when a school district in Maryland hired me as a highly qualified teacher. 'Highly qualified' meant I had the schooling and experience, but would be trained to become a certified teacher. I took the required exam for teachers and passed all parts except the math, which I later retook and received a passing grade. I moved back to Maryland and began my training at Johns Hopkins University in June 2004. I took the necessary classes toward certification for middle and high school. My first assignment was sixth grade at an inner city school. Again I was confronted with the mis-education of the inner city children. I was expected to make it look like something really wonderful was happening at that school. No one seemed to care that many of the children were years behind their grade level. This was truly an overwhelming experience.

I had difficulty dealing with the behavioral issues. My experience in today's classrooms caused me to know that every classroom, at least through eighth grade, must have two adult bodies. If educating each child is primary, teachers need help with the behavioral problems. Moreover, there was a certain kind of persona you had to adopt in order to effectively teach in those inner city school environments. I could not manage to play the part. My principal once told me I had a 'Sunday school face'. The harsh tactics that I observed inner city teachers using to get African American children's attention was not easy for me. My health was being compromised. Therefore at the end of the second year, I quit.

The emotional turmoil at this period in my life was indescribable. I was menopausal, but did not pay much attention to that aspect. It was only on looking back that I realize the significance menopause had on my emotions at that time. I was also dealing with adopting a new paradigm for living. One morning, while at a point of great indecision, I began packing with the intention of giving up my apartment. While taking the books out of the case I picked up *Demian*, by Hermann Hesse. I could not put it down. Between those pages I found assurance. Though written many years before, this book assured me that I was not alone in questioning the myths of the world we live in. A few days later I went to the library and requested all that Herman Hesse had written. From the large selection I chose to read *Siddhartha*. It is amazing how the universe gives you just what you need at the right time. In this book Hermann Hesse spells out the hero's journey and the lesson learned along the way. I was in the baby stage of living from the perspective of my True Self. *Siddhartha* contributed significantly to my understanding and spiritual awareness.

That summer I did not know how I was going

to keep my apartment and support myself. I don't know if you can call it providence, but my car was hit from behind and I collected a $10,000 insurance settlement which took care of my needs that summer. As a result of the accident, I had to have chiropractic care. It was the chiropractor and my primary care physician that recommended I find another job for my health's sake.

As the new school year dawned, I received a call from the new principal asking me to return. Under the illusion that because of new management, things were changing at the school, I returned that September. I lasted until February. Mentally and physically, I could not deal with inner city teaching. Truthfully, one of the issues I faced was the amount of time teaching consumed, particularly, teaching social studies. Since social studies is mostly reading and writing, there were always projects to oversee and papers to read. I finally concluded that teaching was just not my calling.

In February of 2007, after leaving my teaching position, I gave up my apartment in Baltimore and moved back to DC to live with my son for a short time. He had bought a house with the teacher next door and I lived on the third floor. The time spent with my son should have been enjoyable, but it was not. Although there was some aspects of my presence he enjoyed, like my cooking, and house cleaning, as a single young man he was uncomfortable living with his mother.

It was then that I began writing this book. Writing at that time was cathartic. I was able to leave many of the issues that bugged me on those pages. After finishing ten chapters, the USB storage drive broke. This was the only place I had it stored. I became desperate to find someone who could retrieve my pages. Through an internet search, I finally communicated with the gentleman in Dallas who had retrieved the data from the space shuttle Challenger. He agreed to help me for five hundred dollars. I paid him in increments. After I paid him four hundred dollars, he sent me the CD. That same year I went to Barbados. When I returned, my luggage with my computer inside was stolen out of my son's driveway. Along with that loss went my desire to continue writing.

One month after leaving the teaching position, I was hired by a research company in Rockville

Maryland and trained to be a field representative for a prominent American health organization. The job required me to travel to different states, make cold calls and do health interviews. I worked full time hours when on the job, but the position was temporary. I so wanted it to be a full time job, but that never happened. I loved the job. I met some interesting people along the way. I never met a stranger, so this was an easy job for me. Not all the people I met were nice, some even lied to my co-workers when the occasion arose for a follow-up call. Ironically, the respondents that complained about me were African Americans. One African American male travelled twenty minutes to visit the temporary local office to tell the office manager: "you not only send someone to my house, but you send a foreigner."

I really believe that my cultural difference contributed to my not forming close relationships with any of the ladies on the team. God knows I tried. I thought I was building a relationship with the woman assigned to mentor me. She too got very upset with me when we were in New York. She called me to her room to share a video of a woman beating up a man that someone had sent her. She thought it was very funny. I saw no humor in it whatsoever. Before that incident, when we first arrived in New York, we went shopping together, we did the sauna at the hotel together, and I was happy to be making a friend. However, after the video incident she stopped communicating with me. I missed her.

True to form, I tend not to draw a crowd of friends; instead I usually gravitate to one person to develop a lasting relationship. Whenever I arrived to a new site I always inquired as to who was there and would call to greet them. No one did that for me. If I was passing and saw some of them congregating in the hotel lounge areas I always stopped to visit and chit chat. If they stayed in my building, I would knock on their hotel room door to say hi.

Shopping was the favorite pastime of some of my coworkers. My big goal was to save as much money as I could, therefore I did very little shopping. I was on a mission to be rid of the debt I had acquired when funds were low. Furthermore, because of my hypertension, my doctor voiced his concern about me taking the job. He understood how easy it was to eat unhealthily when living out of a suitcase. I was not concerned because going out to eat was not what I preferred. Although I received a per diem, I chose to go to the supermarket and make my own meals. Most of the time there was a Whole Foods or Trader Joe's close to where we were staying. We mostly stayed at Residence Inns, which made cooking possible. When we stayed in a regular hotel, there was always a fridge. I then ate salads and good artisan bread. This was for me the healthiest way to live.

After the assignment in Greensboro North Carolina ended in May 2008, I was sent home. I had a gut feeling that this was my last assignment and I was right. They had called back to work an African American who had worked for the company before. Their policy was to have as few African Americans as possible. I was in the process of moving to Charlotte for the second time, so I went to my daughter's house. Eventually, after many attempts to get in touch with the head manager of the project, she called me in July to tell me she did not need me anymore. She said: "You are no good." Those were her exact words. Although I knew that she had not dealt with other workers equitably,

I never thought I would be treated like that. In my estimation I had done a good job. I had no way of knowing how I was failing their expectations, and I was never given a review. I felt like I was used and cast away, as she had done with many others. According to her, my coworkers had made damaging complaints about me. They said I was a very angry person and I was not a team player. These complaints flabbergasted me, because I thought I helped when the need arose. Furthermore I had been told by the site manager that the head office did not like buddying up. His words were: "you must always work separately."

On the first assignment in Wilson, North Carolina, the new female full-time recruit would come to my room for help to understand how to do the work. When we went to the conference in Los Angeles, I drove another co-worker from the airport to the hotel and back, since she did not want to drive the car that was readily available for her at the airport. When I made special food I would share. I am a very passionate person and at that time I was still sometimes dealing with depression. Perhaps, if my co-workers had cared enough and did not let what they thought were my peculiarities influence them, they could have gotten to know me better. They would have observed that I am culturally different. I am a very strong Caribbean woman who likes my own space. Could that make me anti-social, perhaps? As I look at the older women in my family, I find a similar trait. They have a lot of acquaintances, but they don't buddy up.

I think the bias against me started when we were training. We stayed in Rockville, Maryland. One evening, I decided to go with them to dinner. I was alone in not wanting crab cakes. I don't eat any kind of crustacean. I didn't mind going for crab cakes, but to drive all the way to Baltimore just for a crab cakes was preposterous as far as I was concerned, when there were so many wonderful restaurants in the Rockville and the surrounding areas. It was only when we got on the way that I realized we were going to Baltimore, and I was not pleased. I felt I was hoodwinked into going to Baltimore. After all that, at the end of the evening, the consensus was that the crab cakes were not good. Would I have eaten out more if I had known that not socializing would cause me to lose my job? No.

One of the women I trained with asked me if I had experienced a catastrophic illness that caused me to be so particular about my food. From my teenage years I understood the correlation between eating well and growing old gracefully. Furthermore, I come from a culture that cooked all the food we ate. Going out to eat was not the thing to do in Barbados when I lived there. The majority of food served in America's restaurants has hidden sugar and salt, a very good reason to eat out less. I will always make the choice to eat well. Even though I am not an Adventist any more, that is one aspect of their teachings I took with me. In my opinion, it has worked for me. No one can guess that I am as old as I am. The evidence of the gossip about my peculiarity became apparent when I invited a male coworker for dinner. He said: "you are very nice." His comment came over as a surprise. The gossip had him expecting something very different.

Although working for the research company did not last long, I have wonderful memories of the amazing people who let me, a total stranger, so willingly into their homes. Most memorable are the ones that after much resistance, I was able to get them to change their minds and participate in the survey. Sometimes those hard to get ones became my advocates in their community.

I was now sixty years old and once more without work. This was not how I hoped my life would turn out. I had no medical insurance. My only income was the small unemployment check I was able to qualify for, since I was sent home before I was fired. However, I was not afraid, for by this time I had a cursory understanding of who I was in relation to our existence. Hence I knew I would be taken care of. Furthermore, I still knew how to spend money wisely.

Earlier that year while on break from the survey job, a good friend made it possible for me to pay only four hundred and fifty dollars for a seven-day cruise to celebrate my sixtieth birthday. The ship stopped in Barbados the day before my birthday and my mother made a delicious lunch to celebrate with a few of my friends who live in Barbados and a few relatives. Although arranged on short notice, it was really special to celebrate this milestone with my mother. How was I to know that two years later she would become very ill and die?

This was the time of the economic downturn and many people my age found themselves jobless and fearful for their future. Having made lemonade with my lemons all my life, this is what I did in Charlotte. I moved into the condo I unsuccessfully tried to buy from my son-in-law, and again began the task of job hunting. To supplement my unemployment check I applied for food stamps. It was a wise thing I had done in saving as much money as I could, for it enabled me to set up house, even though I did not have a job. I shopped at the thrift shops for my furnishings. The only thing I didn't need was a bed and a dining room table. In fact, I started thrift shopping while I was still working in Greensboro. While on the job I bought a beautiful head board for fifteen dollars, I bought a lovely dresser for seventy-five dollars, I paid seventy dollars for two end tables and sixty dollars for a table and five chairs. I only needed the chairs, so I left the table. I refinished all that stuff and I am still enjoying the use of most of it. I had such good rapport with my respondents that one of them picked up and transported the furniture to my daughter's house for the price of gas and lunch.

I had chosen not to keep a car while I was traveling for the survey job since they always provided a company car. Therefore, when the job ended, I was without a car and was even prepared to use public transportation. Fortunately, one of my daughter's co-workers was selling her old Toyota and with my aunt's help, I bought it. It served me well and it is still serving my granddaughter. Meanwhile, I kept busy helping my daughter maintain seven condos she managed for a friend in New York. I did small repairs, painted and even laid ceramic tile. I never shied away from hard work. During this time I was also completing a course in metaphysics I had started when I was on the work site in Detroit. I was motivated to take this course because I was convinced that I wanted to have a voice in the new conscious direction our world is taking.

I completed the Master's level of that course and wrote a thesis entitled "ONENESS: Society's Sure Fix." As I researched and read for this course, I gained further understanding as to how delusional our world is. Clarity came from authors such as Bruce Lipton, Gregg

Braden, Bishop Spong, Marshal Rosenberg, Adyshanti, Wayne Dyer and many, many more. I was now moving further and further away from the traditional understanding I was raised with, and there was no going back. I knew I was going out on a limb and I heard from some of my relatives that I "needed Jesus". However, I feel that I now have a more profound understanding of who Jesus really was. I now know that the story so concretely built around him was just a retelling of stories that could be found in earlier literature, such as Gilgamesh. If there was such a man, I believe he understood and lived a life in harmony with his true self.

The meme that sounds like such profound truth serves to stop many from understanding the real truth. As the waves are one with the ocean, so we are one with 'What Is' or what man calls God. Thus we are empowered. However, we have been disempowered by the teaching that we are wretched sinners. Give a man a name, and he lives up to it. Our society certainly demonstrates what we have been taught to believe. Even Jesus was purported as saying "The Kingdom of God is within you." And again, "do you not know that you are Gods?" He also said, "greater things than these you will do…" Was he a madman? He obviously knew that the same innate power that was within him is within us. I believe this old paradigm has run its course; it is time for a new paradigm. Who lives up to it anyhow? The unconsciousness of our world is beckoning for us to become a more loving, compassionate people. I know that we can only become this by doing away with all dogmas that separate us and get to know who we truly are. There is amazing freedom in this understanding. There is freedom from judgement, freedom to love generously, and freedom to be truly compassionate.

Not having a job had its advantages. I was available to spend time with my grandsons during the summer months. I took them to the library and made sure they read. They probably were not happy, but they will remember the summer grandma took them to the library and to the parks. Being available also enabled me to be present when my college friend had two major surgeries. The second time I was the only one there for her, and I was happy to serve her. I was also available when the time came for my mother to be cared for.

In 2009 I went home for Christmas. Going to Barbados regularly to see her was important for me. She was what Barbados signified for me. As soon as I saw her that November, I knew she was not well. She had aged fifteen years since I had last seen her. This was particularly evident when she was around other heathy people. Our relationship had always been superficial. She was my mother and I appreciated her, but the kind of relationship some daughters have with their mothers, I did not have with mine. I was a 'mistake' even 62 years later. I was also a mistake that caused her much pain. Indeed, I was continuing to cause her pain by moving away from the religion she had taught me. My opinions were of little value to her and her immediate family, her husband, and my two brothers. As I observed her deteriorated state, on two occasions I diplomatically tried approaching the issue of her health. One of those times she said to me: "I live here with a husband and son and they don't see anything wrong with me. Why are you saying that something is wrong with me?" This pained me. I walked away from the house and cried.

Eventually Ma went to the doctor. That day when she returned she said to me, "Dr. (Fake) told me to go home and eat my food, you don't have any cancer." I said to her "Ma, who told you that you have cancer?" Was he blind? Did he not see how the flesh was just melting off her body? Did she tell him she was having severe night sweats? One doesn't have to be a doctor to recognize when someone's health is failing. I am no doctor, but if she had told me that, I would have known that something was wrong with her liver.

Actually, she had visited the doctor because of my cousin's persuasion. Since she would not listen to me, I talked to both her niece and nephew whom she willingly served when they asked. I was curious to know if they did not observe that she was not herself. Both of them then admitted that they noticed some difference, and it was her niece who persuaded her to see the doctor. In reality, she asked Ma to get another opinion. When Ma discussed the idea of getting a second opinion, my stepfather didn't see anything wrong with her and that was the end of that idea.

As providence would have it, my journey

back to America was in transit through Toronto. Since my brother lived there, I asked for a longer layover. At the time I did not know how significant that layover would be. I then took that opportunity to talk to my brother about Ma's failing health. Meanwhile, shortly before I left Barbados, I sent a picture of her to her brother in Canada and her sister in Florida. They agreed with me that she seemed in failing health. My aunt waited until I left to call her. She told Ma I sent a picture and it appeared as if she was ill. She then urged Ma to seek medical help. By this time Ma had admitted to herself that she was not well, and was willing to go back to the same fool who she had seen just a few weeks before. It is unbelievable how much confidence she had in this doctor. All he ever did was give her stronger medicine. He never even did blood work to see if the medicine was affecting her in negative ways.

When Ma went back claiming a pain in her side, he sent her for a CAT scan. The results of the test finally came back positive. Ma had cancer. I returned to America in January and by March Ma needed critical care. When I heard of the results of the test, being her oldest and her only girl, I felt it was my place to return and help her. When I called and told her I wanted to come back, she said, "I don't need you here, I have a husband. He took care of me when I was sick years ago and he will do it now." Once again, I was pained by her words. I felt rejected one more time.

My oldest brother who lives in Canada eventually went home to assess the situation. Then he called to tell me I needed to get there as soon as possible. I gladly returned in April to care for my mother. The rapid decline was unbelievable. Just months before she was fussing, telling me, to prove that she was not sick, how much more work than all of us she could do. Indeed at her age she was still catering to all of us. However, I did notice that she was willing to let me help her more when I was home for Christmas. I was even surprised that she let me cook her Christmas dinner. As I watched her attending to her many duties I found myself wondering when she was going to be catered to, for she would have been eighty that year. Ma died six weeks after I returned. All she said to me was: "Laine, how did you know?"

I have no doubt that my mother loved me. Living out of her conscious understanding, she did for me the best she knew how. The following is what I said at her funeral:

We are here to honor the memory of a martyr. If Ma was Catholic I would recommend that she be considered for sainthood. I know many of you here have seen the commercial for Duracell batteries that keep going and going and going. Ma reminded me of that commercial in that she just kept giving and giving and giving. Her spirit of service to everyone was remarkable. Even on her death bed she continued to be more concerned about the well-being of others than about herself.

Undoubtedly, Ma taught me many things, she did so knowingly and unknowingly. I learned from her in life and even at her death. I learned from her how to be and how not to be. I learned from her the importance of faithfulness, dedication and commitment. When I was only 2 months old she joined the Pentecostal church and she never wavered in her commitment to her Christian faith. Most importantly, as a woman, I learned from Ma the importance of self-actualization. In other words, I learned the importance of knowing and giving to self.

The essence of Ma continues to exist in her children and grandchildren. Only this week,

243

someone called the house and I answered the phone. After talking to me she called her sister and said, a woman answered the phone who sounded just like Sister Carmichael. As Ma's only daughter, I have already passed Ma's torch on to my two daughters and my daughter who has 3 daughters are in the process of doing the same. Hence, who Ma was will continue. Today, though saddened by Ma's passing, I am assured that Ma is resting in peace.

I returned to America not knowing when I would return to Barbados. Ma was gone and with her the home in Barbados I so looked forward to visiting. I did return to Barbados the very next year in August for the funeral of another female martyr. This time it was my ex-husband's sister. She did not live to see her sixtieth birthday. Many women spend their entire lives just giving and giving to husbands and children to the detriment of their own health. I too was on that journey until I came to my senses and understood that if I didn't care for myself, no man would, or could.

While I was in Barbados for my sister-in-law's funeral, I was hired by the Charlotte public schools as a substitute teacher. Since I could not find a job, I was forced to take Social Security at sixty-two and was wanting a job that would supplement it. I like substituting because I could work as much or as little as I wanted too. While substituting I continued to manage the condos. In the meantime, every weekend I volunteered at the Performing Arts Center in Charlotte. This was the best volunteer job, since I got to see and hear performances without having to pay.

Although I was happy to get out of my marriage, I knew I did not like being alone. I was not unhappy being alone, but I knew the value of companionship. While married I had often said that I was never going to get married again, but I later found out that that was the circumstances talking. I had a great desire to find a mate. One thing I was sure of though, I was not remarrying for marrying's sake. During the many years I was single, I dated. I sometimes dated men who were not available physically and many who were unavailable emotionally. I joined the social media dating scene and encountered some gentlemen and some real jerks. I even dated a Syrian who was a real wolf in sheep's clothing. His only interest was winning me to Islam. He eventually concluded that he never met anyone like me.

Unfortunately for him, I was through with any kind of organized dogma.

During those days in Charlotte, in addition to my work I did yoga, attended spiritual meet-ups, hosted spiritual gatherings and in 2008 I adopted a dog named Charlie. Charlie is a cross between a Pomeranian and a Chihuahua. He is the cutest and most loving little thing. He is also a very hyper little fellow. In observing him, I realized that trying to get him not be hyper is like trying to get a baby not to cry. It is who Charlie is, very excitable. In observing him, I've gained greater respect for my own passionate type 'A' personality. Also, observing Charlie's capacity to give love and receive love caused me to understand how children can never get enough love. And like Charlie, they will accept love from whoever gives it.

I was very happy in the little condo on Oak Meadow Lane. I painted every room in restful colors. I planted flowers in the front and in the little space in the backyard, I planted tomatoes, cucumbers and squash. Charlie and I were really at peace in our home. Charlie was known and loved by many of the people in the development. I had made many acquaintances and a few friends. I was good friends with Gordon. We met while walking our dogs. His two, Midnight and Shadow, always wanted to stop by my gate and it seemed that Charlie always knew when they were passing. I took care of Shadow and Midnight when Gordon travelled and he returned the favor with Charlie. On Thanksgiving of 2011, Charlie and I drove to Florida to visit my aunt. I intuitively realized that my aunt needed help. She was dealing with her husband who had Alzheimer's. I understood that at eighty years old she was carrying a great burden. I offered to move there and help her, but she was not open to the suggestion. As he progressively got worse, she became accepting of my offer. I gave up my comfortable space and on October 27, 2012 Charlie and I moved to Clearwater, Florida.

FOURTEEN

Freedom

*"Your vision will become clear only when
you look into your heart. Who looks outside,
dreams. Who looks inside, awakens."*

- Carl Jung -

AS I contemplate my past experiences, the failed relationships, the many jobs that did not last, particularly the ones I liked, I can state emphatically that none of them was in vain. I alone created them all to teach me the lessons I needed to learn. Without them the understanding I now have clarity about would not have been possible. Yes, many times as I was living the experiences I questioned why, and I often felt that in spite of my capabilities I was such a failure. Adding to this feeling were the disparaging and negative comments that came from the people who were closest to me.

My brother said to me when I had lost one of the jobs: "I told my wife you were not going to last in that job." That spoke to his negative opinion of me. I find so little compassion from so-called successful people. In their estimation, they made it. They make the big bucks, drive the big cars, live in the expensive houses, so everyone can and must do the same. I suppose because of my experience, I have a compassionate understanding for those less fortunate. Can we all follow the same path? No. If we all succeeded to the same degree who will get to practice the South Africans' Ubuntu? Ubuntu is a practice of sharing that connects all humanity. It demonstrates the understanding of the 'Oneness' of our existence.

If I were a career woman with great responsibility, chances are I would not have been able to go home and serve my mother in her final days. Neither would I have been able to volunteer to move to Florida and help my aunt. A friend of mine always said to me: "Rose, you value what is important." On the top of my list of important things is good health and next to that is a willingness to serve how and when

I can.

My eldest grandson and my eldest son moved me to Florida. I rented a U-Haul and they took turns driving it. I felt so blessed to have a grandson who was willing to drive his grandmother to Florida. He actually did most of the driving. It took us about twelve hours, but we made it without incident. My grandson flew home a day later and my son stayed for a few more days. Little did I know that those few days with him at my aunt's house would be the last time I would see him alive.

I made the decision to move to my aunt's house from a heart place. My aunt and I had a very close relationship, so I believe. I told her everything. I was more intimate with her than I was with my own mother. However, the day I walked into her house I had a premonition that I had not made the right move and I said to my son: "What have I done?" What loomed before me that day was, I am still my mother's child and although I was willing to give up all and come to help, I would always be secondary to my aunt's children. Can you believe that at 65 I was still yearning to belong? The reality is, my thought did not come from nowhere, my ego was remembering.

The six months I stayed with her were good. I received a small salary. Therefore, in addition to helping with my uncle, I cleaned house, tended the garden and my presence gave my aunt freedom to go and do what she had to do. We always knew that my stay at her house was only temporary. But I needed time to recoup some of the thousand dollars I spent for the move. I did look for and applied for a few places within my budget. The apartment my aunt liked and would have preferred me to live in was above my budget and I had no intention of being a slave to an apartment. I submitted a few applications at places I could afford. I finally received one response to my application months later when I was settled in my current home.

Shortly after I moved to Florida, I began attending a Unitarian Universalist church. It was there that I met the first friend I made in Florida. The first morning I visited was her first morning there in a long time. She lives in Italy. She was home to visit her mother. We found camaraderie and eventually I staged her mom's house after she went back to Italy. As a result of my staging, one of the first people to look at the house bought it. Staging that house was a monumental task. It was more than staging. The house was a cluttered mess and with my friend's help I de-cluttered, did small repairs, stripped wallpaper and painted in order to show off the potential of the house. I would wake up early in the morning and go there before the sun came up, working until it was almost time when I would be needed at my aunt's house. This was not an easy task, but it gave me a little extra money.

While attending another social function at the Unitarian church I learned about a walking group. I found it on the Meet-Up site and joined. The first Saturday morning in January when I went walking was when I met Harry, or I would say Harry met me. He walked with me that day and he talked my ears off. He was going through a personal, painful time and I guess he was needing to talk to whoever would listen. As I listened to him that day, I knew I was listening to someone with a heart. Furthermore, it was readily apparent that we were from the same kind of strict Christian background. I must have given him my information, for early the next morning I received a text with a telephone number. I replied to it by saying "this must be Harry," and it was. After that we walked together every Saturday morning. He took me on dates to the beach, to happenings in different local towns and even to one of his friends' birthday parties. We also met in beautiful Philippe Park every Wednesday night to walk and then go out for dinner. Our relationship developed fast. I think it was because we were both at a crossroads in our lives.

Harry was in the process of his third divorce and I was being forced out of my aunt's house. She needed the space just in case her daughter and great granddaughter came to visit. I liked Harry. To many he was a high risk because he'd been married three times before. In my estimation, the opposite is true. It is the man who flits from woman to woman without a commitment that is the highest risk. Furthermore, as Harry talked about the three cats his wife and stepchildren were forcing him to adopt, I knew for sure this was a man with a heart. Most men would have quickly taken those animals to the pound. He willingly kept them and lovingly cared for the three; now he cares for two, because one died. He also lovingly cares for my dog Charlie. Charlie shows his love for Harry by getting unbelievably excited when Harry returns home from work in the evening. If Charlie could talk, he would ask me where Harry is when between 5:30 and 6:00 pm Harry is not home yet.

I came to realize that although it was Harry's idea to meet and walk on Wednesday night, he was often very tired. So after a while I started making the forty-five minute drive to his house and staying until the next morning. Harry and his house offered me what I was wanting, a secure partner with a house. I dreamt of planting food and flowers and even having my own chickens. Living in Florida was the next best thing to living in Barbados, where the weather was conducive to gardening. Four months after we met we decided that I would move into Harry's house. I had my trepidation. After all, Harry had just gotten out of a relationship and I questioned him about getting into a relationship on the rebound. He assured me and I believed him. The result of moving in and living with Harry is the stuff you read about in story books.

In June 2010, I wrote a list of aspirations. The following is a copy of that list:

This is what I aspire towards:

- Finish my thesis and get my Master's in Metaphysical Counseling
- Find a place/job where I can truly minister to my fellow man.
- Finish Africans in the Americas: Yes WE Can.
- Help my grandchildren through college
- Be continuously peaceful
- Be able to go to the chiropractor on a monthly basis
- Be able to have monthly massage
- Drive a newer car/Toyota or Honda
- Live in a home with a place for a garden and chickens
- Live in a 3 bedroom, 2 bathroom cottage with porches in front and back
- Have a loving, giving, spiritual partner, who is emotionally and spiritually grounded

Today February, 12th 2015, I just found that list. Number three and four are the only things on that list I have not accomplished. Harry has afforded me nine, ten and eleven. His house is exactly what I aspired for: three bedrooms, two full baths, a linai in the back and a nice little porch in the front, where we sit and look out on our garden, for we turned the front yard into a beautiful garden that gets all the attention from those who pass by. Chickens are too much of a liability. We like to travel and chickens would add constraint. Growing in our garden are many of the things that grow in Barbados: pigeon peas, avocado, mango, Barbados cherry, and paw paw trees. This summer I will again plant sweet potatoes, okras and Barbados yam.

Humans are peculiar. We ask for things and when they come we doubt. Shortly after I started interacting with Harry, I asked him: "who are you?" His answer was, "what you see is what you get." I had difficulty believing he was as good as he is. I didn't say he is perfect. Harry truly is a loving, giving, spiritual partner, who is emotionally and spiritually grounded. I was never in a relationship with anyone where there was such ease in the relationship. There was a time when I would not have recognized these qualities in Harry. I would have wanted and expected him to reflect his truth the same way

I do. I now understand with great appreciation that he reflects his truth in his own way and I love him. As Gary Zukav states in The Seat of The Soul, when referring to his spiritual partner, I love being in love with Harry.

Moment by moment I live with a deep sense of gratitude. In my school of life the lessons were not always easy, but as I look back many people came to my aid and for them I am very grateful. Particularly, in my time of economic need, sometimes without asking, many of my relatives contributed. My uncle in Canada, my aunt in Florida, my brother in Canada, my cousin in New York and the one who now lives in New Jersey. There was a time when I was homeless and friends in Delaware opened their homes to me. Often when we are experiencing challenges we don't see how the way will be made, but on reflection we are amazed at the end result. If we only truly understand that we are an integral part of this universe and as the birds of the air and the flowers of the field are cared for, so will we. With this assurance we will struggle less and the end result will be the same.

I am grateful for my children. They are my

primary teachers. Raising Claudette, Catherine, Erwin and Everett will always be the job I am most proud of. I now have ten healthy, beautiful grandchildren. I have six grandsons and four granddaughters. All the boys are now young men. Can you imagine all that testosterone in one room when we get together? I feel so blessed. I tell people these are my riches. Long after I am gone from this manifestation, I will live through these children. In my limited understanding I gave my children my all. I didn't always have the material things to give, but I taught them values. Everett in particular needed this since he spent all his school days in public school. I would tell them that life's best things cannot be bought or sold, they are truthfulness, kindness and integrity. I also instilled in them to do whatever work they did diligently, even if it was sweeping the streets, for their work was a reflection of themselves.

Today, my oldest daughter is a vice president at one of America's leading banks. She has two sons and a stepdaughter that factors into my number of ten. Often, when Claudette first moved into the management job at the bank and I called her and listened to the greeting on her phone, tears would well up in my eyes. My thoughts would be, boy we have come a long way. Back in my teenage struggles I never could have imagined her success. Her work ethic is what promoted her, for others were looking and recommended her when she was not aware.

My second daughter, though a nursing graduate of Georgetown University and a Captain in the United States Army, chose motherhood as her profession. She has six beautiful children, three boys and three girls. It is her oldest that moved me to Florida. She home schooled all her children for varying periods. It was from this experience that I truly appreciate home schools. Children learn so more and so much more in depth than at public schools.

My eldest son, the fly in my ointment, whom I loved dearly, died in May 2013. He taught me the most. It is from him I learned unconditional love. He was my most brilliant child. He was an amazing chef and a great communicator. In fact, he was a food artist. He not only could cook, but he knew how to present the food. Unfortunately, he began using crack in his thirties and was never able to rise above it. He died at the age of 45. There is more about him in the book about him. He left me a grandson, for which I am most grateful. When I talk to Arysse, I think I am talking to my son. His mannerisms so mirror his father's. Only this past July I met a granddaughter who Erwin relinquished 21 years ago when her mother married to someone else while she was pregnant. In my heart I always believed I would meet her. My heart is full of gratitude for being afforded that opportunity. She is tall, elegant and smiles just like Erwin. She and Arysse are noticeably siblings.

My youngest, my giant son, always big, always strong and particularly strong-willed is a successful teacher of Spanish in Washington DC, and this blesses my heart. I cried many tears as a result of the challenges he presented as a strong-willed child. I am grateful for the wisdom I was given to be able to help him grow into the wonderful human being he has become. He is still strong-willed, but if you get to know him you will find he has a big heart. He married in 2014; no babies yet, but they are coming. He calls me daily and it pleases me as I see my son evolve in awareness of his true self and endeavor to live his truth.

The most taxing years of my adult life were while raising the four individual souls who came here fully packaged. All they needed was to be lovingly guided into their own truth. I know that now. I did not know it then. Like most adults we believe our children are empty slates and thus it is our responsibility to fill them up. As adults we treat children with very little respect as a result of our ignorance. Hence we continue to perpetuate life's heartaches. Can you imagine if we treated children as they grow up as if they had important information to offer? Then we would talk to them and not at them. We do this because most of us believe that because we are adults we have all the answers. We all live from our own conscious understanding. When we know better we do better. I observe many children are being born visibly more aware, my hope is that the parents of these children would be wise in dealing with these individual souls.

The continuous peace that my soul longed for in 2010, I now experience. It's all about changing perspective. *The After Life of Billy Fingers* says "a change in perspective makes the Universe do a different dance." As I grew in understanding of my true self, the self that never dies and is always perfect, I cast away the regret and became free to love generously and live from a compassionate place—compassion that is only possible because of my experiences. Our world seemingly is in utter turmoil. As man seeks to find answers to the things that confront us, he looks to many places outside himself to find the answers. The reality is, the answer to any of life's issues lies within ourselves. As Eckhart Tolle said, "If god has any reality in this world it cannot be separate from who you are in your essence. Who you are beyond form, beyond time."

Our formless self, what some call the soul, never dies and it is always perfect. It is not perfect because of any action on our part. Our failure to be aware is the only way we can be separate from this perfection. The lie we have been told is that we need to save our formed self. We can never save our formed self, it is through the formed self that we can experience our formless self. Our formless self is like the wind. We cannot see it, or touch it, or smell it, but we can know it is there. We all have had intuitive experiences that we marvel at. Those far and few experiences can become our norm, as we commit to consciously living with full awareness of who we truly are.

The commitment to walk in full awareness of who we truly are empowers us. We become aware that the power and majesty of a sunrise or sunset is ours. We don't have to grovel in the mud like beggars. Instead we can affirm what is already ours. In our true essence, we are one with all that is. Call that essence what you may, God, Buddha, Krisna, Divine Oneness, the result is the same. The infinite power whereby we live is too big to be concerned with what name man chooses to use. Does that mean we and our everyday experiences are perfect? No. However, the more we live in awareness, the greater the formed experience will be. We are spiritual beings in human forms.

Finally, I am grateful for the freedom of being that the understanding of who I AM has given to me. My desire for everyone is that they too will experience the peace that's beyond understanding.

GLOSSARY

ackee

the Barbadian ackee is small, green and round and differs from the Jamaican ackee. It is also known as 'guinep' or 'Spanish lime'

coolie man

an immigrant of East Indian ancestry who would ply his trade from house to house and supply wares on credit to householders

dunk(s)

small round berries about 3/4 inches in diameter. The fruit is green and turns yellow as it ripens. Ripe fruit may occasionally develop a rust brown colour and a cracked texture

joiner shop

during the late 20th century much of Barbadian wooden furniture was hand-made by joiners who were sometimes also referred to as carpenters. The joiner specialised in making furniture and structures which required the specialised crafting of wooden 'joints'. Joiners would set up their workshops in small wooden structures along the road, referred to as the 'joiner shop'

licks

a casual way of referring to a spanking or a beating

pipes

water taps situated outside of the home, usually in the yard or on the roadside

Ubuntu

A South African ideology focusing on people's allegiances and relations with each other